FROM

CHAOS

TO

CALM

Simple Habits to Declutter Your Home and Mind

BY AMELIA SAGEWOOD

Paperback ISBN: 979-8-9926575-6-2

Hardback ISBN: 979-8-9926575-7-9

For permission requests or inquiries, contact:
The Awesome Readers

www.theawesomereaders.com

ABOUT THE AUTHOR

Amelia Sagewood is dedicated to helping people create balance, clarity, and calm in their daily lives. With a focus on practical strategies for decluttering both the mind and the home, she empowers readers to simplify their routines, reduce stress, and embrace a more intentional lifestyle.

Her books combine gentle guidance with actionable steps, offering readers the tools they need to let go of overwhelm and make space for what truly matters. Whether it's clearing mental clutter or creating a peaceful home environment, Amelia's mission is to inspire lasting change through simplicity and mindfulness.

When she isn't writing, Amelia enjoys quiet mornings with a good book, long walks in nature, and the simple joy of an organized, peaceful space.

YOUR EXCLUSIVE ACCESS

Thanks a million for being here. Your support means so much to me!

The best way to keep in touch with me is by signing up for my newsletter –
https://theawesomereaders.com/

Or scan the QR Code below

See you soon,

Amelia Sagewood

TABLE OF CONTENTS

INTRODUCTION

Your alarm goes off. Too early. Maybe just ten more minutes of sleep . . . Snooze. You finally roll out of bed and trip on the pile of clothes laying on the floor. Are these the clean ones that you meant to fold last night? Hard to tell. You need your morning coffee, but there are no clean mugs and the sink is overflowing with dishes. Starbucks it is.

Gotta shower before your work presentation. This towel is probably good for another use, right? Hope for the best. Get in the shower and knock over the 12 shampoos, conditioners, body washes, and bath bombs on the ledge. You don't have a bathtub yet, but hey, it never hurts being prepared.

Gotta get dressed. Your closet is full of clothes, but you don't want to wear any of them. You're kicking yourself for wearing your favorite shirt yesterday. A few minutes later you find serviceable attire.

Time to pack your lunch. Nope. The fridge is packed with food you don't have time to make, besides the Tupperware is still in the sink. There's a good burrito place close to work anyway.

After a couple minutes of scrambling to find your keys, you walk to your car, go to sit down but first you have to move the napkins from yesterday's fast-food dinner from the driver seat. You catch a whiff of something. . . Is that a gym bag? Not sure how long that's been there. Thankfully it's warm enough to ride with the windows down.

You get to work a couple minutes late. The line at Starbucks was longer than anticipated. You get to your desk and see the mountains of paperwork calling your name. You definitely have a system, but good luck teaching it to anyone else. You start by answering emails. 1,773 UNREAD. Yikes. Let's get to it. After making a dent, you better check your socials. And your news sites. And your texts. While you're taking a break, you might as well get that second cup of coffee.

Almost time for your presentation. Which folder are your notes in, again? You have three and they are all overflowing. You feel a little underprepared, but the presentation goes smoothly enough. Your boss, impressed, offers you a chance to take the lead on a new project. You don't ask any questions and say "yes" on the spot.

After a few more hours of paperwork, emails, and phone calls, you get back in your car and head home for the night. You need some dinner, but after your big presentation you don't have it in you to wash the pots and pans in the sink, use them again, and put them back in the sink to be washed. Maybe tomorrow. Tonight sounds like a good night for Chinese food. You eat Chinese take-out and stream your favorite show.

It's time for bed, but they end the episode on a cliffhanger. You tell yourself that you just want to watch until you get resolution. We'll see how that goes.

You finally crash into your unmade bed, scroll for a bit, then pass out until your alarm goes off again tomorrow. You hope tomorrow is a better day, but your expectations are pretty low.

Does this sound familiar to you? This is a picture of a cluttered life. A life that has too much stuff with no system to manage it. A life lacking intentionality. A life that is reactive instead of proactive. A life where you feel more like a passenger than a driver. A life where hurry and anxiety is the default setting. There is a better way to live.

In this book we will explore ways to push back against the chaos of clutter that continuously creeps into our lives. Even if it feels like you are drowning and don't see any way out, there is hope. This is not a book about radically changing your life. It is a book about habit and mindset shifts that, over time, lead to a lighter and more purpose-driven existence. The steps themselves are not radical, but the transformation you will experience is undeniable.

I am indebted to BJ Fogg, author of *Tiny Habits* and James Clear, author of *Atomic Habits*. They both show that taking small, consistent action over a long period of time is better for long-term success than big sweeping goals and changes. We might have great goals and desires, but we will always be limited by the quality of our systems.

For example, it would be better to say, "I will wash one dish after I finish dinner" than to say, "I will never go to bed with dishes in the sink ever again." If you frequently have a sink full of dishes, moving to zero dishes is too much change too soon. When you inevitably miss a night, you will likely get discouraged. When you get discouraged, you lose momentum and stop believing that progress is possible. The motivation you had at the start will inevitably fade as the difficulty increases.

Fogg notes that motivation and willpower are notoriously unreliable (Fogg, 2019). There is a reason that 90% of New Year's resolutions fail by February. Maybe you watched a show about tidying up or saw a sleek post on Instagram that made you yearn for a clutter-free lifestyle. You then have a grand plan of knocking it out in a weekend. Maybe things go well for an hour or two, then you get to the closet, or that one drawer that has been collecting random odds and ends for years. You slowly lose steam and start questioning if it is even possible for you to live with less clutter. I want you to know that change is possible! You just have to go about it the right way. Let's consider the mechanics of behavior.

ON BEHAVIOR

For you to do any behavior, you need motivation, ability, and a prompt. A seemingly demanding task requires a lot of motivation, whereas an easy task requires little motivation. Our brains love a shortcut. There are things that we want, and we want to get them as quickly and easily as possible. It is no wonder why we are addicted to things like technology and junk food. They give a big dopamine hit with minimal effort. See the image of the behavior model below:

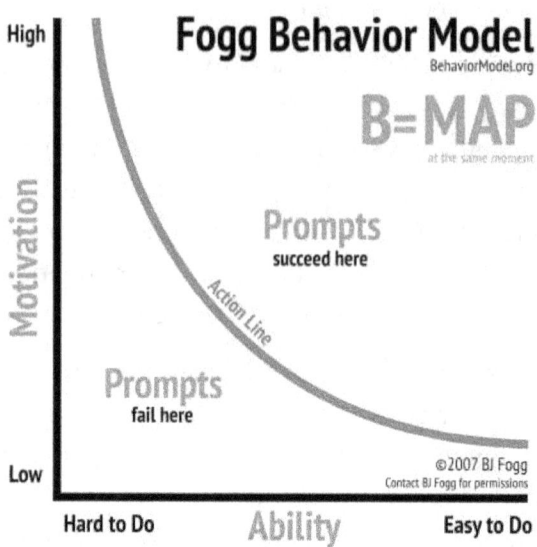

High | **Fogg Behavior Model**
BehaviorModel.org

$$B = MAP$$
at the same moment

Prompts
succeed here

Action Line

Prompts
fail here

Low | ©2007 BJ Fogg
Contact BJ Fogg for permissions

Hard to Do | Ability | Easy to Do

A hard task is anything that requires more time and mental, physical, or emotional effort than you want to spend. Doing difficult tasks requires motivation, which, as we discussed above, is unreliable. How can we ever get ourselves to do hard things when we can't rely on willpower?

The key is to take a difficult task and make it easier and/or shorter. Folding a full basket of laundry feels hard to do and I usually don't have the willpower to do it. However, folding clothes for two minutes feels a lot easier. Who knows? Maybe after two minutes I will be in the zone and finish the whole bag anyway. Or maybe I stop after two minutes and the laundry is 17% less chaotic than it was before I started. Washing a sink full of dishes is a lot. Putting one bowl in the dishwasher is simple, easy, and requires very little time. It is also true that tasks get easier the more we do it. Maybe you don't like folding laundry because you never learned how to do it well.

The prompt is perhaps the most important part. The prompt signals to you that it is time to do the task. Hunger pangs signal it is time to eat. A phone vibrating signals you to check your text messages. Boredom might prompt you to scroll. In order to effectively build good decluttering habits into your life, you need a reliable prompt. Start by pairing your new habit with something you already do every day. For example, maybe you clear the bathroom counters while brushing your teeth since that is a task you already do twice a day. Or maybe you put clothes in the laundry basket when you get undressed to shower instead of leaving them on the floor.

BJ Fogg encourages us to remember our ABCs: "After . . . Behavior . . . Celebration." After an established habit occurs (prompt), do the tiny version of the new habit you want to embody (behavior), and celebrate in a way that makes you feel good. Positive emotion releases dopamine, and makes us crave the behaviors that we are rewarded for (even if we reward ourselves).

It is often the case that perspiration comes before inspiration. This means that you have to start a task before you feel motivated to do the task. Any writer will tell you that writing is the only way get over writer's block. In order to write a masterpiece you have to consistently do the work of writing below-average work until true genius arrives. Similarly, as you consistently take small steps in decluttering, you will begin to crave a clutter-free life. With a little guidance and planning, you can systematically remove clutter from your life and keep it away for good.

KEY IDEAS

Here are a few key ideas and mindsets that will serve as the foundation for our decluttering process:

EVERYTHING HAS A PURPOSE.

William Morris, an English textile designer in the 1880's said, "Have nothing in your houses that you do not know to be useful or believe to be beautiful." Holding on to things that are no longer useful or beautiful to you is one reason for the clutter in our lives. It is essential that the items we keep serve a positive purpose in our lives. If they don't, they need to go. As you go room by room, ask yourself, "Does this item improve my life, or is it holding me back from the life I want?" Marie Kondo's method is to physically hold each item in your house and ask, "Does this item spark joy?" If it doesn't spark joy, it is removed.

EVERYTHING HAS A PLACE.

Cutter also occurs when useful things are not in their proper place. Dishes in the bedroom, clothes on the floor, wrappers on the counter are all examples of things that are out of place. Finding a home for all of our possessions is crucial in winning the war against clutter. For many people, it is difficult to find a place for everything because they have too much stuff. Too many books for the bookshelf. Too many shirts for the drawer. Too many dishes in the cupboard. Removing items is the most effective way for finding space for your possessions.

I am also indebted to *Organization for Dummies.* This book teaches the acronym PLACE to help you transform chaos into order. It stands for:

Purge- Get rid of anything that is not useful or beautiful.

Like with Like- Group similar items together when you deciding a place for your possessions.

Access- Make the things you use more frequently easy to access. Make things you use infrequently, or desire to use less, harder to access.

Contain- Drawers overflowing would be the opposite of contained. When things are out of sight, they remain out of mind. Inversely, things that are in sight stay in your mind. Keeping items contained frees up mental space for important things.

Evaluate- Decluttering is a journey, not a destination. There will always be things you can tweak to make more efficient, effective, or aesthetically appealing. Seasons change. People change. Circumstances change. There will be times when a previous arrangement no longer serves your needs. Be willing to give an honest evaluation of what is working and what isn't.

UNDERSTANDING THE CYCLES

Many things in life follow a never-ending cycle. Night turns to day and back again. One season gives way to another, year after year after year. Similarly, our possessions have a life-cycle. Some items were made for single use, while other items can be used until they break down. For single-use items the cycle is very short: use it and get rid of it. Clutter then comes when things don't get thrown away in a timely manner after they have served their purpose. Things like wrappers, paper towels, and empty cans would fit into this category.

The simplest cycle for reusable items is: use it and put it back. Think of a toy or hairbrush that doesn't need to be washed between uses, for example. Clutter comes when they don't get put back away. They still have a purpose for you, but are out of place. There are more complex cycles for things like dishes, laundry, and trash/recycling that we will explore more in Part 2.

In Part 1, we will explore the effects and reasons for the clutter in our life and mindset shifts that help us break free.

Part 2 gives guidance for decluttering your kitchen, living room, bedroom and bathroom. We will explore what the purpose is for each space and practical steps you can take to remove clutter.

In Part 3 we will examine the nuances of paper and digital clutter, as well as organizational and storage solutions.

In Part 4 we will explore daily, weekly, and seasonal habits that will equip you to keep the clutter at bay for good. For now, we will turn our attention to the negative impact of clutter on our lives.

PART I:
DECLUTTERING MINDSET & MOTIVATION

CHAPTER 1:
THE EFFECTS OF CLUTTER

Have you ever walked into a room and immediately felt overwhelmed by the amount of things strewn about? Whether it is a pile of clothes, a sink overflowing with dishes, or a trashcan that is overflowing, you get the sense that things aren't what they should be. A house is meant to be a refuge to get away from the storms of life. However, clutter is often a way that the chaos of life penetrates our safe havens.

Dr. Joseph Ferrari, a professor of psychology at DePaul University defines clutter as "an overabundance of possessions that collectively can create chaos and disorderly living spaces." Another way to think about it is that clutter is an obstacle that is between you and your goal. If your goal is to find your keys, the pile of junk mail hiding your keys would be clutter. Dr. Ferrari has found that there is a negative correlation between life satisfaction and clutter. The more clutter you have, the lower your life satisfaction. Here are some of the ways clutter negatively affects us:

Mentally: Not only can chaotic environments sabotage our productivity, they also heighten anxiety and stress levels, and impact our sleep. Each disorganized pile acts like a miniature volcano, simmering with potential eruptions of worry and tension. Research even shows that clutter can trigger a persistent fight-or- flight response, keeping cortisol perpetually elevated (Sander, 2019). A meaningful life is one in which you can focus on the important things of life. Clutter robs you of the focus. Also, the longer clutter builds up, the harder it will be to deal with, meaning we will need even greater motivation to address. As you procrastinate guilt and anxiety builds up.

Financially: The average American carries around $6500 in credit card debt. In the first quarter of 2025, the total American credit card debt reached a record high of $1.1 trillion dollars. Debt like this leads to lower credit scores which makes it even harder to get out of the financial pit. Not only has overconsumption led to debt, it is also extremely difficult to contain. In 1974 the median house size in America was 1,560 square feet. In 2024, it was 2,146 square feet. Despite housing being 500 square feet larger, about a third of Americans need to rent a storage unit, an additional $50-250 per month.

According to another study, Americans have over $7,000 of unused stuff in their house. That is almost two months of wages just taking up space. Our addiction to consumption means working more hours to pay for it. Which brings us to the next impact of clutter.

Time and Effort: The more possessions you have, the more time and effort it takes to manage. A bigger yard means more time raking leaves and mowing the grass. Every additional bedroom is another bed to make and floor to vacuum. It takes half as long to fold ten shirts than twenty shirts. Opting for more is robbing you of the one resource that is non-fungible: time. You can make more money, you can replace most possessions, but you can't buy more time (no matter how hard billionaires try). Joshua Becker recounts the moment that led him to become a minimalist. It was a normal Saturday and Joshua spent the day cleaning the garage. His son begged him to come play, but Joshua was too busy. It was in that moment that he realized his stuff was keeping him from being present with the most important people in his life. That sent him on a journey to radically live with less. You only get one life. How do you want to invest your precious time and energy?

Relationally: Relationships can be hindered by clutter in a variety of ways. Maybe the amount of clutter in your home dissuades you from hosting friends and family. Maybe you have to work more hours to pay off the credit cards you used to buy all your stuff. Maybe you can't wind down with a glass of wine with your partner at the end of the night because there are too many chores to get done, plus you are too tired from working the extra hours. Maybe you are incapable of saying no and spread yourself too thin to have deep connections with anyone. You become an inch deep and a mile wide. Maybe the amount of possessions you inherit from a deceased relative lead to feelings of resentment that they left you this Herculean task to manage.

Tyler Durden summed it up well in *Fight Club*, "Advertising has us chasing cars and clothes, working jobs we hate so we can buy [stuff] we don't need, and the things you own, end up owning you." We buy the thing. Get insurance for the thing. Maintain the thing. Worry about the thing. Regret the thing. Feel guilty about spending money on the thing. Maybe a newer model is what you really need . . . This is the trap of consumerism.

We can clearly see the negative impact clutter has on our lives. It is not as easy to see how our lives get cluttered in the first place or why it is so hard to become clutter-free. That is the topic for the next chapter.

CHAPTER 2:
THE REASON FOR CLUTTER

Your life is a cluttered mess and you feel stuck in an environment that isn't life-giving. How did you get in this situation? There was not one thing that led to your cluttered life, rather, millions of decisions, indecisions, and unconscious habits over the years brought you to where you are. The good news is that since you got yourself into this mess, you have the ability and responsibility to get yourself out. You are not destined to live this way forever. You can make changes to your life. Still, it is helpful to understand why our lives get cluttered in the first place.

The simple answer is because too many things enter your home and not enough exit. We buy things, are gifted things, inherit things, and borrow things. Some things get delivered to your home without your permission (I'm looking at you junk mail). Our homes are like a sponge soaking up possessions. The problem is they never get wrung out. It is so easy for things to come in, but it is much more difficult to let them go. Have you ever considered why we buy the things that we do?

Obviously things we buy vary based on our culture, family of origin, what we can access, and some social conditioning. However, a common thread is that everything we buy promises to make our lives better in some way. People buy expensive dumbbells because they promised to make them fit without having to leave home. Some believe that buying a new pair of running shoes will finally motivate them to become a jogger. Different clothes serve various functions. Some clothes promise comfort (cozy sweat pants), others promise status, a means of telling the world what type of person you are. Many things promise to make our lives easier. Some promise to make us more productive, others more attractive. Some promise joy and entertainment. Why you buy certain things depends on what type of person you want to become. "Where your treasure is, there your heart will be." Our possessions are a window into our hopes, dreams, desires, and values. You might say you value one thing, but your spending habits reveal the truth.

It is easy to understand why Americans struggle with consumeristic tendencies. We are inundated with ads from a young age. We see consumerism in the movies and shows we watch. All of our friends are doing it too. It is simply the water we swim in. However, it is more difficult to discern why we hold on to things longer than we should. I believe they fall under four broad categories: fear, fatigue, inaccurate self-image, and sentimentality.

FEAR

There are different fears that keep us from letting go.

There is the fear of not having enough. "What if people come over and I don't have enough mugs? What if I only keep one item and it breaks?"

There is the fear of disappointing others. "This was a gift. What will I tell them when they ask about it? What if they come over and realize that I got rid of their gift? Will that offend them and damage our relationship?"

The fear of regret. "What if I get rid of this and end up wanting to use it in the future?"

The fear of forgetting. "What if I get rid of this picture of my grandfather and I don't think about him anymore?"

The fear of being wasteful. "I spent $100 on this. If I get rid of this item it will be like I'm throwing money away. I haven't used this item in years, but I better hold on to it just in case."

What fears hold you back in your decluttering journey?

MENTAL AND EMOTIONAL FATIGUE

The more possessions we have, the more decisions we must make. Decision fatigue often follows. Imagine starting your morning wading through a pile of mismatched socks to find that one elusive pair. By the time you're done, you've used up precious decision-making energy, leaving less for other important tasks.

Decision fatigue is like running out of steam before getting started on your big decluttering project. When faced with too many choices, our brain's ability to make wise decisions deteriorates. As stated by Rita Wilkins (Downsizing Decluttering, 2024), "Psychology Today estimates that we make more than 2,000 decisions each working hour." Our mental stamina is continuously tested. The more choices we face, the faster we exhaust our cognitive reserves, causing frustration and leading us to avoid the process of decluttering. When we don't have the mental capacity to declutter, we tend to procrastinate.

Procrastination is a formidable opponent in the battle against clutter. Understanding why we avoid decluttering is the first step towards overcoming this obstacle. Often, it's not the task itself that we dread, but rather the mental barriers and emotional responses triggered by clutter. These triggers vary from person to person. For some, the sheer volume of possessions can be overwhelming, leading to paralysis. Others may fear making decisions about what to discard, worrying about future regrets or sentimental losses. By recognizing these personal avoidance patterns, one can start to dismantle the reasons behind procrastination.

Sometimes decluttering feels like opening up Pandora's box. Maybe there is a drawer, file cabinet, or closet that you refuse to examine because you know once you take things out you won't be able to contain it. Or it is like a hydra. You cut off one head and immediately two more grow in its place. Maybe it is the items themselves that are emotionally draining. For example, maybe you inherited the possessions of a loved one who passed away and you aren't ready to process all of the memories and deal with the inevitable grief that comes with it. Or the clothes and makeup that bring up insecurities that you would rather not deal with. In the short-term, it is easier to avoid the hard feelings and push them off, but as we saw in the previous chapter, keeping clutter around has many negative consequences.

INACCURATE SELF-IMAGE

We often hold on to things that reflect who we want to be or used to be rather than who we are now. Maybe there are clothes in your closet that haven't fit in years, but you just know that this is the year that you will get back into shape. Maybe there are books on your shelf that you bought with good intentions but know deep down you will never read. It is hard to admit that you aren't the type of person who reads *Crime and Punishment* in your free time. I have a bicycle and bicycle shoes that I haven't used in four years, that I won't let go of. Biking was a big part of my life in high school and college, and I don't want to fully close that chapter of my life. I also have idyllic visions of biking to work, going on family bike rides, or even doing a triathlon someday. To get rid of my bicycle is to admit that I am not a biker anymore. I'm not someone who likes to show up to work dripping in sweat from the ride over. I also fear that I will regret selling the bike and then kick myself for wasting money when I buy a different one in the future. Decluttering forces us to be honest about who we are and what is important to us. No wonder it feels so difficult.

SENTIMENTALITY

In our quest to declutter, we often find ourselves held back by unseen forces of nostalgia and emotional ties. These bonds shape the very essence of why some items persist in our lives despite their apparent lack of utility. Imagine a dusty old book that sits on your shelf, covers worn and pages yellowed. You don't read it anymore, perhaps you never truly enjoyed it. Yet there it remains, untouched, always spared from the donation box. Why? Ah, it's because that book was gifted by a long-lost friend during a summer filled with discovery and laughter. It's not about the book, but the vivid memories it resurrects.

Nostalgia is a powerful influence. It colors our perception of objects, imbuing them with emotional significance far beyond their actual use (R.D, 2024). As humans, we find comfort in tangible reminders of past experiences. They serve as portals to cherished moments and bygone days. This sentimental attachment complicates our decluttering efforts, even when those items are otherwise useless.

But sentimentality isn't just about revisiting happy memories; it also reflects our self-image. That hand-me-down sweater from college, threadbare and unfashionable, might symbolize our adventurous spirit or youthful ambition. Letting go feels like erasing part of our identity (Burger, 2023). We're all curators of our personal museums, where each item represents a chapter of our lives. This makes the decluttering challenge deeply personal and often fraught with internal conflict.

We have explored the complex reasons for how lives become cluttered and why it is so difficult to escape. In the next chapter we will consider how to break free.

CHAPTER 3:
BREAKING FREE FROM CLUTTER

In the previous chapter we discussed reasons why it is so hard to rid ourselves from the clutter in our lives. When we declutter, we come face to face with our true selves. So often we hide behind our things. When we declutter, we declare with our actions what is most important to us. We untangle what we really want from what others expect us to want. A young woman who considers paring down her makeup must confront the possibility of making herself vulnerable by presenting a more natural face to the world. "What if I'm not attractive enough?"

Parents might hold onto baby clothes for nostalgia's sake. Or they might not be ready to admit that they are done having kids. To get rid of the clothes is to admit that you will never bring another child into the world. It is hard to admit that the newborn stage is done forever.

Doing the work of decluttering is comparable to doing the work of therapy. Both require you to be honest about who you really are. Both require you to confront your past and dream about your future. If done right, both will bring tears. It also makes sense why decluttering is so challenging. Let's consider the things that hold us back from decluttering that we discussed in the previous chapter and how we can overcome them.

FEAR

It is impossible to overcome fear without acknowledging it. An unseen enemy is when it is most dangerous to you. You can't get over your fear without admitting, with as much specificity you can, what it is you're afraid of.

Ask yourself, "What am I afraid of?" You can then ask yourself "why?" until you feel like you are as close to the core as you can get. At the root of almost every fear is a lie. Lies give fear their power. The only way to defeat a lie is with the truth. Here are some examples:

Maybe someone acknowledges that they are hesitant to declutter because they are afraid of not having enough. I would follow up by asking, "Enough to, what? How much is enough? How do you know when you've arrived at 'enough?'" They have likely never considered these questions.

They discern that the financial instability they experienced as a child has them terrified of being poor again. What might they do with that realization in the context of decluttering? It will take a lot of internal work, but they will have to shift from a scarcity mindset to an abundance mindset. A move from "I don't have enough" to "I have everything I need." They might take an honest look at their current financial situation, craft a plan for building up an emergency fund and getting out of debt. Having an emergency fund gives you some margin if you somehow declutter too much and find yourself needing to re-buy certain items. Here are some other potential lies:

LIE: "I can't get rid of the TV because I am afraid that I will be bored and miss out."

TRUTH: People existed without TV for most of human history. The TV is likely keeping you from living your adventurous life because you are stuck inside watching other people's adventures.

LIE: "If I get rid of so many clothes people will notice that I'm frequently wearing the same clothes."

TRUTH: Most people are so self-conscious that they don't pay attention to the things that you are self-conscious about. Even if it is something they notice, it will eventually just become a part of your style. You will also feel better about what you wear by only keeping the clothes you love.

LIE: "How am I supposed to host my friends if I get rid of these plates?"

TRUTH: How many people do you expect to have over at once and how often? Do you host people now, or is that something you wish you could do? Can you get paper plates? Can you ask a guest to bring some? What if you rented plates for one day?

LIE: "My grandma gave me this sweater. What if she notices that I don't have it anymore?"

TRUTH: It is unlikely that she will notice, but even if she does, you can respectfully tell the truth. "That sweater was such a thoughtful gift. It just didn't work for me and I found somebody who could get more use out of it. I love you and appreciate you thinking about me."

What fears hold you back from letting go? What might be the lie that you are believing?

MENTAL AND EMOTIONAL FATIGUE

Maybe you like the idea of decluttering, but you feel like you don't have the time or mental or emotional energy. What then? Here are a few tips:

Start Small- Maybe you start with a single drawer, one section of the counter, or the front seats of your car. The goal is quick victories. Hopefully it is a space you use often so that you can feel the positive difference it makes in your life. Professional organizer Vicky Silverthorn suggests starting with something as ordinary as a sock drawer. Empty it out, identify what's worth keeping, categorize, and voila! You have not only organized a space but also gained confidence to do more (Silverthorn, 2018). Tackling small tasks provides quick wins that build momentum and instill a sense of accomplishment that fuels further efforts.

A step is a small thing on its own, but if you put enough steps together you can climb a mountain.

Start Easy- I recommend that you don't start with sentimental items. Those require a sense of discernment that you discover in the process of decluttering. Start with the things you don't have much emotional attachment to. Also, don't start with difficult spaces like the attic, garage, or basement storage room. If you are just getting into running, you don't start with a marathon. Maybe you do a 5K, then work your way up from there. The same principle applies. Start with the kitchen counters or a comparable space. Marie Kondo recommends starting with clothes. After that move to books, papers, miscellaneous household items, and then sentimental items. After enough repetition you build up your decluttering muscles to the point you are capable of tackling the tougher areas.

Make it a Habit- Habits are our brains' way of navigating through an infinitely complex world. When a habit is established, your brain signals to your body what to do, and you can unconsciously perform the task. Consider driving a car. When you first learned to drive you were conscious about every turn, every time you pressed the brake or accelerator. After a few years of driving, you perform all of these tasks automatically. This is great news if we have good habits! It's not such good news with habits we are trying to break.

BJ Fogg points out that any behavior (B) requires motivation (M), ability (A), and a prompt (P). The formula is B = MAP. Motivation is unreliable. It will be high one day and non-existent the next. So, a great way to start a new habit is to directly connect it to an established habit. For example, every morning I make coffee using a French press. I'm a coffee addict, so it would take something very strange happening for me not to make my morning coffee. Making French press coffee requires me to boil water and allow the coffee grounds to steep for five minutes. My decluttering habit attached to my coffee addiction is to unload the dishwasher and/or wash pots and pans while I wait for the coffee. I no longer have to think about when to do the dishes. It is built into my routine. When I first built this habit, I started with washing one dish. As the habit became more established, I instinctively increased the number of dishes I washed. Then I got to celebrate with a delicious cup of coffee!

Habits can either be a great defense against decision fatigue or they can lead you into a deeper mess. When healthy habits are established in the rhythms of your life, success almost becomes automatic. When there are unhealthy/unhelpful habits such as compulsive online shopping, doom

19

scrolling social media, or leaving clothes on the floor our lives become more cluttered and chaotic.   .

INACCURATE SELF-IMAGE

Every person has a gap between who they are and who they want to be. To take it further, every person has a gap between who they are and who they pretend to be in front of others. We are all works in progress. We all have flaws and shortcomings. Things that we are ashamed of. Often this shows up in our possessions. Maybe there are things you bought to fit in or impress someone else. Maybe you bought something out of an insecurity. Maybe there are possessions that you hold on to because they encompass the life you want instead of the life you have. In order to make progress in your decluttering journey, you must be radically honest about who you are and what you want most in life. I have heard it said that your life is perfectly designed to get the results you're getting. When you are honest with yourself you can redesign your life to fit what you truly want.

Not only do you have to be honest, you also need to come to the place of self-acceptance. Shame is a terrible motivator, positive emotion is always more powerful. It's okay that you aren't the same size you were in college. It is okay that you don't have the "right" hobbies. It is better to do things you actually enjoy than to keep the things that you pretend to enjoy, or believe that you should enjoy, when you really don't. I'm not saying that you shouldn't strive to grow. We all need to grow. What I am saying is that our possessions are not the way we grow. Oftentimes our excess possessions hold us back from growing into the life we were made to live. Time spent cleaning when you could be working out. Time spent working when you could be spending time with family. When we declutter, we learn what is most important to us. When we do that we find our true selves.

SENTIMENTALITY

Why do we hold on to so many things from the past that we never look at? On my bookshelf are many journals that I filled in the years after college. I don't think I will ever read them again, yet I can't bring myself to throw them out. Why? Maybe I have delusions of grandeur and want to save something for my future biographer? Maybe I will digitize it someday and have it organized so I can easily access my brief moments of brilliance? I think the real reason is that it feels like a part of my soul is within those pages. Maybe for you it is old clothing, or a gift from a deceased loved one that you never use, but can't let go of. Nostalgia is a powerful influence. We tend to attach memories to the physical objects. Letting go feels like erasing part of our identity (Burger, 2023). This makes the decluttering challenge deeply personal and often fraught with internal conflict.

To tackle this, it's essential to understand these attachments, allowing us to distinguish between memory and physical presence. Objects may have played a role in our lives, but they aren't the memories themselves. Realizing this can be liberating. The memory will persist, whether or not the object stays. Reflecting on the value of experiences over objects can significantly ease the process of parting with possessions. Our lived experiences are much richer than the material clutter we accumulate.

This doesn't mean purging every piece linked to a fond remembrance. Rather, creating balance is key. Consider the concept of a "memory box." Think of it as a curated collection of your life. Choose a modest-sized box and select only the most meaningful keepsakes to fill it. By limiting the space, you naturally curate your belongings, ensuring that only the most treasured items make the cut (Burger, 2023). This tactic not only preserves space but encapsulates your narrative more meaningfully.

When considering what belongs in this box, ask yourself guiding questions, such as "Does this evoke joy?" or "Why am I holding onto this?" If an object genuinely captures a moment of happiness or symbolizes a significant aspect of your life, then into the box it goes. Otherwise, it might be time to let it go. Such reflective questions empower decision-making and clarify the value of keeping or releasing specific objects.

Decluttering, then, becomes less about eliminating clutter and more about honoring memories. It allows us to maintain a sense of connection without drowning in possessions. So, as you sift through bookshelves and drawers, allow yourself to reminisce, but don't lose sight of the practicality of space. Embrace a philosophy that treasures memories above materials, recognizing that sometimes, the story is better told in whispers rather than shouts. Also, there is power in keeping the sentimental items that you keep on display. They aren't enriching your life in any way when you keep it in a box in the attic. As you declutter other items, you make space for important sentimental items to be on display.

WHAT IS YOUR WHY?

Nietzsche once said, "He who has a why to live for can bear almost any how." Having a good enough reason for decluttering will provide added motivation to persevere when things get overwhelming.

Why do you want to declutter? Are you tired of misplacing your wallet and keys? Are you frustrated that you constantly feel rushed when it's time to leave the house? Do you feel a sense of dread when you get home rather than a sense of peace? Do you want to travel more? Be more hospitable? Be a good example for your children? Do you want to be more focused and productive? Do you want to spend more time doing things you love with the people you love? Do you want to get out of debt and find financial freedom?

Whatever your reason, make it clear and visible to keep motivation high. A simple yet powerful practice is the creation of a vision board—something that serves as a constant reminder of what you hope to achieve by getting rid of excess clutter (admin, 2024). Vision boards serve as tangible reminders of your goals, bringing them to life through images and words that inspire you. Gather photos, clippings, and drawings of spaces that embody your dream environment. Create a collage that encapsulates this vision and place it somewhere you see often—perhaps on the fridge or next to your desk. Each time you glance at the board, you reinforce your motivation to declutter, knowing every item you let go brings you a step closer to that ideal space (*11 Decluttering Motivation Tips: Useful Guide - EZ CleanUp*, 2024).

When you know your reasons for decluttering, you're not just tossing out old clothes and forgotten trinkets; you're opening up space for better things to come.

What is your why? Take some time to reflect on that question before we discuss tips on decluttering your spaces/.

PART II:
QUICK WINS FOR EVERY SPACE

So far we have discussed the negative impact that clutter has on our lives and ways that we can overcome it. We will now get down to the business of decluttering your space. We will go room by room and give a step-by-step decluttering guide. Not everything I share will be relevant to your specific living space, but I hope to give you basic principles so that you feel equipped to declutter on your own. You can do this!

Keep in mind some insights from the introduction:

Everything has a purpose. Not only does every item need to clearly add value to your life, every room has a specific purpose. When we have clarity about what a room is for, we have greater clarity about what should stay and what should go. We will begin each chapter by stating the purpose of a living space.

Everything has a place. When everything you own has a designated place, you don't have to spend time wondering where a particular item is. Everything will either be in use or in its place. Things feel cluttered and disordered when they are out of place. But things feel as they should when they are where they should be.

Everything has a life cycle. Understanding the cycles of the things in your home allow you to discern a standard operating procedure (SOP) for your living space. You will also gain clarity about where is the "kink in the hose" or the break in the chain that introduces chaos into your home. You can then "unkink the hose" so that your home runs smoothly again.

Small, consistent habits are more beneficial than sweeping changes. Big life changes are usually unsustainable. Doing a little bit every day is more peaceful in the moment and more sustainable for the long-term. As you read, consider which decluttering tips can be stacked with habits you already do each day. For example, "After I get up from the couch I will pick one item off of the floor and put it away." If you get up from the couch 20 times per day, that is 20 items that will no longer be on the floor. Minimal effort with big results.

PLACE- Purge, Like with like, Access, Contain, Evaluate. I won't explicitly state this framework each chapter, but have it in the back of your mind as you embark on your decluttering journey.

With these things in mind, let's begin in the heart of the home: the kitchen.

CHAPTER 4: KITCHEN RESET: CLEAR COUNTERS, CLEAR MIND

A KITCHEN'S PURPOSE-

When you think of the word "kitchen," what comes to mind? Maybe you see your grandma preparing a family meal. Maybe you think of the fast-paced restaurant workers who bring you a delicious meal for a date night. The kitchen is where the household is sustained. It is for preparing food, eating food, storing food, and cleaning the things you used to prepare, eat, and store food. Take a moment to look around your kitchen. What do you see that has nothing to do with preparing, eating, storing, or cleaning food? These items should be purged or moved to a new location. We'll begin with the counters.

CLEAR COUNTERS

Flat spaces tend to be clutter magnets. We set things down on a flat surface, forget about it, and it stays there forever. Having clear counters is perhaps the biggest bang for your buck in your quest to declutter. It is a relatively simple task, yet you quickly feel the effects. What is on your counter right now?

- **Trash-** Are there any wrappers, used paper towels, empty cans or bottles, or mail that you don't need? Throw them away. This requires minimal thought and effort, but makes a big difference.
- **Dishes-** We will get more into the cycle of dishes momentarily. For now, start by putting the dirty dishes in the sink and the clean dishes away.

- **Food**- Put leftovers in the fridge or freezer and snacks in the pantry.
- **Electronics**- Consider moving phones and phone chargers to a different location since they don't serve the purpose of making food.
- **Paper**- We will deal more with paper in a different chapter. For now, consider should it be recycled or kept? Recycle what needs to be recycled and move what should be kept into a better location, like an office.
- **Appliances**- If possible, put things like toasters, blenders, mixers, and griddles out of sight.
- **Purses and bags**- Find a convenient place to hang.
- **Keys**- Have a designated bowl or hook for keys. Remember, everything needs a place! Consider having a drop zone in your entryway for things like wallets and keys.
- **Loose cash and coins**- Put cash in your wallet and coins in a coin purse, jar, or piggie bank. There is no reason for them to be on the counter.

After the counters are clear, we can turn our attention to our drawers and cupboards, the things we use to prepare food.

PREPARING FOOD

Items that fit into the "preparing food" category are things like pots, pans, spatulas, tongs, whisks, mixing spoons, cutting boards, knives, cheese graters, and certain appliances.

We begin with the P in PLACE: Purge. Throw away anything that is broken. Donate duplicates that you don't need (how many spoons and spatulas do you really need). However, you need to make sure everyone in the house is in agreement about what stays and what goes. I have a friend who almost got divorced because he got rid of a second whisk without asking his wife. The husband reasoned that one whisk would suffice, since it would be unlikely that they would need both whisks at the same time. Unbeknownst to the husband, his wife intentionally bought two whisks. She had many experiences when she needed a whisk, but couldn't use it because it was dirty. Not only did he get rid of a whisk without consulting her, he also got rid of the nicer whisk and kept the cheap, boring one. It took months for them to resolve that conflict . . . Moral of the story, get rid of duplicates, but don't get rid of someone else's stuff without consulting them.

Are there items that you thought would be great for you, but you don't actually use? That air-fryer that you got for your wedding that is still unopened years later? The cake pans you keep even though you have no interest in baking? The charcuterie board that you don't really know what goes on it? What do you gain by hanging on to something that you never use? This is where you will have to mind the gap between where you are and where you would like to be. It is okay that you're not a smoothie person or a star baker.

A rule of thumb is to get rid of anything that you haven't used in the past year. If you went a whole year without it, do you really think you will miss it when it's gone?

You have decided what to keep. Now what? Place like with like. Have a place for utensils. Another for pots and pans, and another for appliances. Remember to keep the things you use most often in a location that is easily accessible. Your future self will thank you for it. It should be easier to keep everything together when there are fewer items.

EATING FOOD

Let's move on to the items you use when eating your food. These would be the plates, bowls, silverware, glasses, mugs. We will essentially go through the same process. Are there items that are cracked or chipped? Do you have 8 half sets of plates and bowls? For these, ask yourself, "How many plates, bowls, and mugs are enough for my stage of life?" A single person can probably get by with 4-6, while a family might need closer to 12-15. Having fewer dishes gives the cupboards a more open feel, and you don't have to worry about glasses falling down because there are too many of them smooshed in the cupboard.

STORING FOOD

The average family of four throws away $1,600 worth of food each year. That is almost two months of groceries in the garbage per year. The clutter in our fridge and pantry is costing us money each month and frustration daily. Here are a few steps to break free:

- Throw away everything that is expired or soiled. You made a mistake by letting the food go bad. There is no need to make another mistake by keeping food you will never eat on the shelf.
- Put the leftovers somewhere easily accessible, like in the front of the shelf in the fridge, so that they don't get lost in the back and go bad before you can eat it.
- Place like with like. Condiments with condiments, likely in the door. Vegetables in the vegetable drawer. Meats with meats, beverages with beverages. Cans with cans. Snacks with snacks. Etc.
- Use what you have before buying more groceries. Maybe you use those cans of corn and green beans with dinner tonight, along with the pasta noodles that have been in the back of your pantry for a year.
- Concerning the pantry, you should attempt to make your pantry look like a grocery store shelf. Like items stacked behind each other, and every product visible. The things you use most should be easily accessible. A well-organized pantry aids in meal planning because you can quickly see what you have on hand and what needs restocking.
- We can't talk about storing food without dealing with Tupperware. Odds are you have too many containers with too few lids. The first step is to throw out anything that doesn't have a lid and any that are damaged. Next, discern how many storage containers your family needs (it is probably less than you think). Growing up we often saved old deli containers and used those to

store leftovers. I am proud of our resourcefulness, but we also didn't know when to let the containers go. Finding a container to store leftovers was always a frustrating experience.

CLEANING SUPPLIES

After enjoying a delicious meal, there is always stuff to clean up. Spills to wipe up, dishes to wash, trash to throw away, and floors to sweep. Under the sink is a good place to store things like dishwasher detergent, new trash bags, cleaning spray, and Clorox wipes. It is especially important to keep the cleaning supplies away from your food. Consider getting a broom gripper to hang up your broom so that it doesn't fall down and make you trip. You might also have a drawer designated for wash rags and dish towels. The same rules apply: throw out any that are damaged, only keep as many as you need, make sure that they are easily contained in the drawer.

Here is probably the right time to mention that your "junk drawer" shouldn't be in the kitchen. I don't really think you should have one to begin with, junk is another word for clutter. But if you need a space for miscellaneous items, the kitchen is not the place for it. As mentioned above, the kitchen is for things related to food. The junk in the junk drawer has nothing to do with food and should be removed or moved to a new location.

DEALING WITH DISHES

Let's consider the life cycle of dishes. Dishes begin in the cupboard or drawer. We then take them out to use them, either to prepare or enjoy a meal. After we use them they need to be washed, dried, and put back in the cupboard or drawer (See the image below).

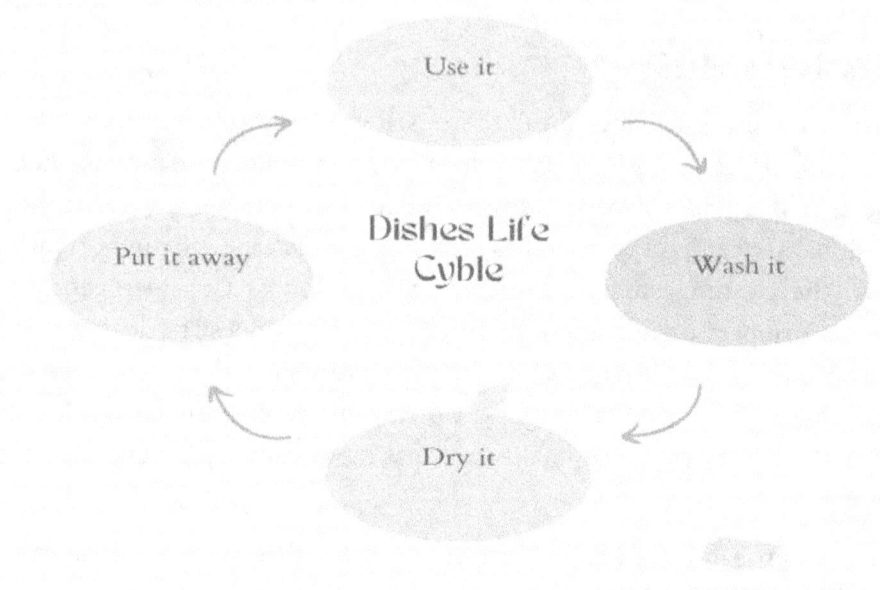

Use it

Put it away

Dishes Life
Cyble

Wash it

Dry it

Chaos ensues when there is extended time between each step. Maybe you leave your glass or plate on the table, counter, or floor after using it. That leaves your space cluttered. Maybe you put the dishes in the sink but don't wash them right away, so your sink gets filled with dishes. A full sink is unappealing to look at and can lead to feelings of dread when you look at it. Maybe you have a dishwasher that you run, but don't unload. This will inevitably result in new dishes overfilling the sink or being left on the table and counter because the sink is full. Maybe you wash dishes, leave them in the dishrack, but don't put them away. This leaves dishes on the counter and adds to the feeling of a cluttered space.

For a more in-depth examination of what to do with dishes, consider this flow-chart:

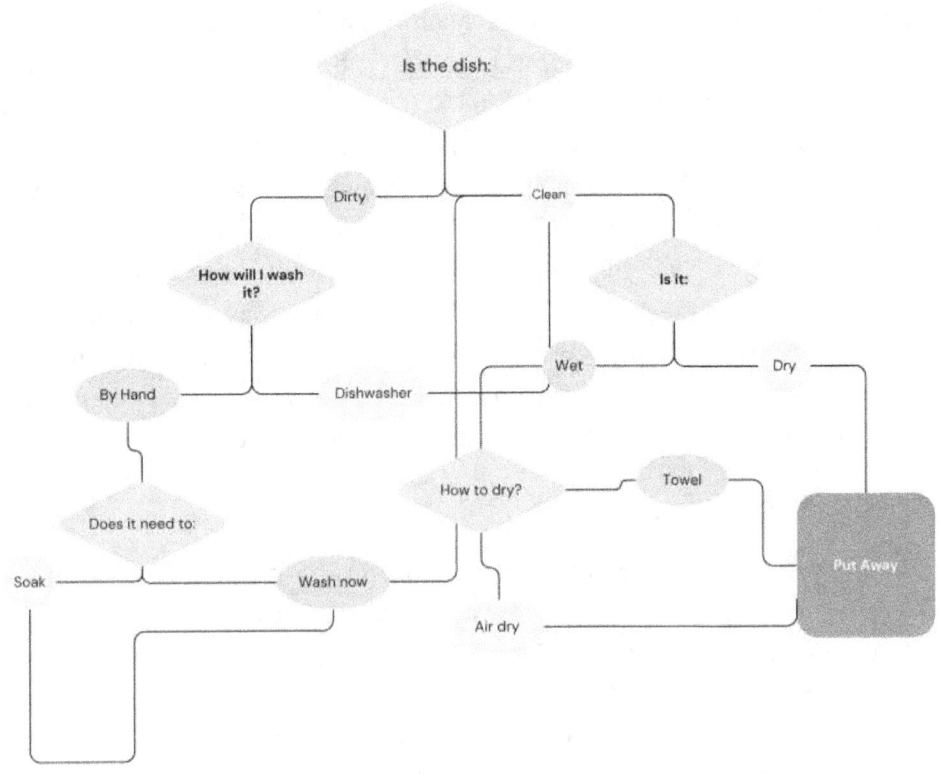

There will always be a trade-off between actions that require time and actions that require effort. The time it takes for a dish to be washed, dried, and put away, is time that you will be living with clutter. For example, it takes longer for dishes to get cleaned using the dishwasher than by hand, but far less effort. It takes longer for dishes to air dry than to use a towel, but air drying requires no effort. Letting dishes soak in the sink makes it easier to clean, but time spent soaking is time when your sink is full. The goal is to find a solution that requires minimal effort, and also results in minimal time spent dealing with clutter.

One solution is to wash dishes at night before you go to bed so that they can dry while you sleep. As mentioned above, I then put dishes away while I boil water for my coffee. I can then load dishes in the dishwasher throughout the day, or let dishes soak in the sink while I'm at work.

The dish always moves from the table, to the sink, to dishwasher/dishrack, to the cupboard again. Our job should always be to take it one step farther on its journey. In your fast-paced life, it is important to celebrate the small wins. If you normally leave dishes on the table all night, it is a win to put them in the sink. Maybe you are diligent about putting your dishes in the sink right away, but it takes you longer to put them in the dishwasher. Your growth step might be putting them in the dishwasher right away. Maybe you are someone who dislikes washing dishes by hand. You can do a couple minutes of dishes at a time, or even wash one dish. By doing this you are slowly pushing back against the clutter of your home and building good habits that will eventually lead to a clutter-free life.

CONCLUDING THOUGHTS

I gave you a lot of information in this chapter, but the important thing is to take things one step at a time. Maybe it takes you a whole week to clear the counters. That's totally fine! Maybe you can only go through one drawer per day. Great! As long as you continually take steps to declutter, you will be forming a space that you will love cooking in. Your motivation can be the meals you get to share with loved ones in your clutter-free kitchen

CHAPTER 5: LIVING ROOM IN MINUTES: MAKE IT WELCOMING WITHOUT THE CLUTTER

The purpose of the living room is right there in the name: live. It is a space for doing things that promote life. It is a space for play, for relaxing, and for connecting with loved ones. But often they end up being spaces that are stressful and uninviting. Because so much happens in the living room, it can become a catch-all, finding things like dishes, wrappers, old homework assignments, stacks of magazines, half-read books, half-done puzzles, and 10 remotes even though you have one TV. In this chapter we will cover books, electronics, furniture, and decorations.

To begin the process of decluttering, begin by removing anything that clearly doesn't belong. Maybe you left the bowl of chips and salsa on the coffee table. Bring it to the kitchen. Did you take your jumper off and leave it on the floor? Hang it up in your bedroom. Throw away any trash that happens to be lying around. Now that the living room only contains things that belong in the living room, we can turn our attention to books.

BOOKS

One's personal library says a lot about who they are. It shows what they are interested in, places they've been, classes they've taken, who influences them, and what they are passionate about. For simplicity's sake, there are two types of books that we own: the ones that we've read and the ones that we haven't. Of the ones you have read, there are those that you will never read again, and those that you will reread or reference in the future. Of the ones you haven't read, there are those that you plan on reading soon and those that you have no interest in reading.

Start by donating those that you know you won't read again or have no desire to read in the future. For example, a college textbook from a class you hated in a field that wasn't your major is a good candidate for being first to go. The old magazines are another that you can get rid of without thinking much about. There will be plenty of grey areas for books that you genuinely want to read but don't know if you will realistically get to them. Don't worry about those yet. Start by taking the easy wins.

Next, consider the space you have available. A good goal is to only keep enough books that can fit correctly on the shelf (standing up with the spine visible, not stacked on top each other or turned with the front facing out).

Sometimes it can be hard parting with books. A helpful tip is to think about specific people to whom you can gift specific books. Maybe there is a fantasy series that you really enjoyed and you have a friend that you would love to talk with about the books. Maybe there was a helpful resource that taught you something interesting about history, politics, money, or technology that would benefit someone else in your life. When we know that the books are helping someone that we care about, we are able to hold them more loosely.

Roughly how many books do you have on your shelf? How many of them do you read in a given year? If nothing changes, how many years would it take you to read every book? If you have more books to read than years that you likely have left to live, it would be wise to get rid of some. Also, moving books into a new living space is always a pain. Your future self will thank you for lightening the load.

ELECTRONICS

Many living rooms have a television. It is a way for families to unwind at the end of the night, or a way to watch your favorite sports team with your friends. It can be a great way to enjoy a shared experience with loved ones, but it can also keep us from meaningful connections. It is difficult to have deep conversation with the TV on in the background. Other electronics you might have are a stereo system, speakers, DVD players, DVDs, video games, cables, and remotes.

Like we discussed with other things, the first step is to get rid of things that no longer serve a purpose. Maybe you don't use your DVD player anymore because you stream your favorite shows and rent movies on Amazon. Do you even know what that tangle of cables are for? Are there video games that are scratched beyond repair? CD's you don't listen to because you get your music from Spotify? Remotes for appliances you don't even have anymore? All of these you can release relatively easily.

Asking other questions like, "What if I got rid of my Xbox to make time to go to the gym?" Or "What if I sell my TV so that I can read more of the books that are on my shelf?" I'm not suggesting that you sell your TV or get rid of video games. However, as you declutter your life it becomes clearer what are the things that are essential to your life, and what are the things that hold you back from what you want most.

FURNITURE

Remember that the living room is for connecting with others. Furniture is a key way to make that happen. Are there any big furniture items such as a coffee table that you don't use? Removing these big items opens up your space in a big way. Maybe your couch is full of throw pillows that end up on the floor whenever anyone sits down. Getting rid of a few of those would go a long way. If you have too many blankets that you don't know where to put, maybe the donation bag is the right spot. Now, what should you do with the furniture that you decide to keep?

Furniture should be arranged in a way that is functional and promotes dialogue. Arranging functional furniture enhances comfort and functionality, setting the stage for seamless social gatherings. Start by focusing on conversation flow. Arrange seating in a way that encourages easy dialogue, such as creating a circle or semi-circle that makes everyone feel included. Opt for pieces that serve a dual purpose, like the storage ottoman with built-in storage to keep things out of sight. At first glance, it seems to be just a stylish footrest or extra seat, but lift the lid, and voilà! You've got yourself a nifty storage compartment. These ottomans are great for tucking away those pesky items that seem to have no home—think remote controls, magazines, or even extra throw blankets. This double duty doesn't just save space; it promotes a relaxing vibe, making guests feel right at home. Ideally, your furniture layout should feel instinctive, guiding people naturally through the room without bumping knees or knocking over lamps. The goal is to have a space that is calm, relaxing, and fun. Having the right furniture and furniture layout are crucial.

DECORATIONS

This is the area that might be difficult for a lot of people because so many of our decorations are sentimental items. The family pictures. The cheesy picture that says "live, laugh, love" that you got from your grandma. The flower vases, candle holders, and things that you got on your last Target run end up filling our walls and surfaces. How do we decide what to keep? How do I know which sentimental item to highlight? To answer these, I want you to think about a museum. When you go to a museum, the walls aren't filled with paintings. Rather, each piece is given its own space, and it goes with the theme of the room. Maybe there is a black and white portrait room, a landscape room, or a photorealism room. The museum doesn't put all of its priceless pieces of art on display, but only what has been curated to fit that specific room at that specific time. We should embody the spirit of a museum curator.

Imagine your living room as an art gallery, where every piece must earn its spot. Curating decor items by limiting them to meaningful pieces not only showcases your personality but also creates a cleaner, more focused environment. Instead of dotting surfaces with knickknacks that might make Marie Kondo break out in hives, choose decor that tells your story. Think of family photos in sleek frames or a statement piece of art that sparks joy. This approach not only minimizes clutter but makes the decor more impactful. You're essentially creating a visual narrative that speaks volumes without saying too much.

What story do you want your living room to tell? Imagine on a coffee table you only have one decoration, but it is an artifact you got on your honeymoon, and you have a wild story about how it came to be in your possession. When there are fewer pieces, people are more likely to notice them, and hopefully you choose things that you find beautiful and love to talk about.

CONCLUDING THOUGHTS

The living room is where life happens in the home. It is where you unwind, have fun, and cultivate meaningful relationships. As you declutter this space, remember that you aren't getting rid of things just to get rid of them. Rather, you are creating a space of connection. A space where you can have a loving conversation with your partner. A space that you love to invite people over to. If you get frustrated in the decluttering process, think about the warm and cozy moments that will be shared in your clutter-free living room.

CHAPTER 6:
BEDROOM SERENITY: CREATE A PEACEFUL, RESTFUL SPACE

The bedroom is one of the most important places in the home. It is where you will spend about a third of your life. Therefore, it is imperative that the space is one that you feel comfortable in. The three main uses for the bedroom are getting dressed, sleeping, and intimacy. Let's see how we can cultivate a space that epitomizes peace and rest.

Similar to other spaces, remove anything that doesn't serve the purposes of the bedroom. Maybe you are a midnight snacker and left plates and chip bags on your nightstand. Maybe there are used tissues or old receipts laying around. Throw away anything that is clearly trash. Maybe you have a habit of working in bed so you leave files or your laptop by your bed. Remove those and put them in an office or similar location.

CLOTHING

Clothing can be a big source of clutter. Maybe your closet and drawers are overflowing with clothes, making it hard to get dressed. Maybe your clothes always end up on the floor. Maybe they stay too long in the laundry basket and you can't remember whether they are dirty or clean. Getting control of your wardrobe will pay dividends for your life. Remember, everything has a purpose and everything has a place. Let's explore some steps for downsizing your wardrobe.

Begin with your sock/underwear drawer. Are there socks that don't have a match? Are there items with holes in them? Are there any items that make you feel uncomfortable when you wear them? Let those go. You can then move on to your other drawers. Remove anything that is ripped, damaged, or no longer fits. Also, if there is an article of clothing that you hate wearing (maybe you dislike how it looks on you or how it feels on you), let it go. You shouldn't hang on to things that make you feel bad when you wear them. With the easy wins out of the way, we can move on to the difficult task of simplifying your wardrobe.

One option is doing the Project 333 challenge. In 2010 Courtney Carver launched the Project 333 challenge. To do the challenge, you curate a wardrobe of 33 items for 3 months (hence 333). The 33 items include all clothing, accessories, jewelry, outerwear, and shoes. Items like sentimental jewelry that you never take off, underwear, sleep wear, or workout clothes do not count towards the 33 items. This challenge may feel daunting to you, but what I appreciate about it is that you aren't getting rid of the clothes forever. It is just a three month experiment to see what it is like to live with less.

Another clothing option is to move to a "uniform." People like Barack Obama, Steve Jobs, and Mark Zuckerberg are some of the modern poster boys for the uniform. They all wore the same thing everyday. Obama wore the same suit. Jobs wore the same turtleneck. Zuck wore the same hoody. They never spent any time thinking about what they would wear for the day, thus freeing up time and mental energy. Maybe it isn't realistic for you to have just one outfit. But could you have five or ten outfits and designate one outfit for each week day? One tip I recommend is to only buy one type of sock. This way you never have to look for a match. Now that we've discussed which clothes to keep, what do we do with those clothes?

Similar to dishes, laundry also follows a life cycle. We begin with the clothes put away in the closet or drawer. You then wear an article of clothing. After wearing it you put it in the laundry basket until laundry day. Then you need to wash, dry, fold, and put the clothes away again. Your space is clutter-free when you stick to this formula, but there are many reasons why chaos might be introduced.

Maybe after wearing clothes you leave them on the floor. Maybe after you take clothes out of the dryer you leave them in the basket. You then realize that you don't have any clean underwear, dump the clean clothes on the bed to find a pair, push the clean clothes on the floor when you stumble into bed, and then realize two days later that you don't know which clothes are clean and which are dirty (not speaking from experience or anything).

The best way to decrease clothing clutter is to put them in the laundry basket right away. Don't ever let the clothes touch the floor! One trick is to keep one laundry basket in the bedroom and another in the bathroom. So often clothes get left on the bathroom floor when you take a shower. Having a second laundry basket helps keep clothes contained.

Another great way to minimize clothing clutter is to fold clothes as soon as possible, but his is easier said than done. Many people dislike folding clothes, and the thought of going through a whole bag requires more motivation than you can muster. One trick is to pair folding laundry with an enjoyable activity, like watching a TV show.

SLEEPING

Getting enough sleep is vital to living a happy, healthy, and productive life. Creating a serene sleeping environment goes beyond just having a comfortable bed. It involves crafting an atmosphere that encourages relaxation and restfulness. One of the first steps to achieving this is decluttering the bedside table. Often, these small surfaces become dumping grounds for all sorts of odds and ends – books, chargers, half- empty water bottles, and abandoned alarm clocks. Getting rid of unnecessary items can significantly reduce distractions, allowing your mind to unwind at the end of a busy day. A clear bedside table might only hold a lamp, a few personal nighttime essentials, or a calming book, creating a soothing space that sets the tone for restful sleep (Slenker- Smith, 2023).

You can also consider getting blackout shades and a sound machine or a fan to help encourage quality sleep. One small decision that has numerous positive effects is to buy an analog alarm clock and go to sleep with your phone in a different room. I can almost hear the excuses now. "You really want me to spend money on something that my phone can already do?! What if there is an emergency?! You expect me to just sit in silence before bed?!"

Calm down. You can get a serviceable alarm clock for around $20. Do you have a legitimate reason why you might expect to receive an emergency call? Maybe a loved one is driving through the night and you want to keep your phone close just in case. That's fine, but it shouldn't be your normal. Lastly, turning your phone off an hour before bed is one of the best ways to improve sleep. The blue light from smartphones delays the release of melatonin, thus delaying our bodies signal to go to sleep. Also, what are you doing on your phone that late at night? Social media and news outlets are designed to make us feel things, usually fear or anger. Scrolling on one of these sites does nothing but rile us up when we should be winding down. Checking email and text messages is another terrible decision before bed. If you don't plan on responding or taking action on any information you see, what is the point in checking? There is a good chance that you will be thinking about how to respond instead of falling asleep. It might even lead to anxious dreams.

Not only is keeping your phone out of the bedroom a great decision for your sleep, it will also help you wake up better. For many people, the first thing they do in the morning (besides snoozing the alarm), is to check text messages, email, news, or social media. Sometimes it is all of them! Before you have even gotten out of bed, the chaos of the world has infiltrated your peaceful space. Think of how much better the day would be if you had a cup of coffee, and spent time reading a book, journaling, or meditating before checking your messages. That life is available to you when you keep your phone out of the bedroom.

INTIMACY

I won't spend too much time on this topic, but it is the reality that if you live with your significant other, the bedroom is where you will engage in consensual activities. When you remove clutter from the bedroom, you remove things that distract you from your partner. To be intimate with another person is to give yourself to them. We can do that most fully when we feel calm and happy. Things that a tranquil bedroom provides. Removing clutter also gives you more time to be with the one you love, since there are fewer things to manage. Who knows? Maybe decluttering will end up transforming your sex life for the better. It can't hurt to try!

TECHNOLOGY IN THE BEDROOM

My partner and I decided that we would never have a TV in the bedroom for multiple reasons. First, we want to set an example for any kids we have. What message does that send if we don't allow TVs in their bedrooms while we have one in our's? Second, a TV in the bedroom would only get in the way of sleeping and intimacy. Think of all the pre-falling asleep conversations we would miss. Think of how many nights we would stay up later than we would have liked because a show was too good.

The bedroom is for getting dressed, intimacy, and sleeping. Technology, outside of a fan or sound machine, does not serve that purpose. And when things don't serve their purpose, they are in the way. They are clutter that needs to be removed.

CHAPTER 7:
BATHROOM BLISS: DECLUTTER FOR EFFICIENCY AND CALM

The bathroom is perhaps the biggest misnomer in the whole house. While it is allegedly known for the bath, it actually contains so much more (and some don't even have a bathtub!). The main components of the bathroom are the bath/shower, toilet, sink, mirror, counters and drawers. The bathroom is for hygiene, beauty, and grooming. It is a relatively small space, so the effects of clutter are amplified.

To begin to declutter the bathroom, we must first remove anything that doesn't belong. The clothes and towels that were left on the floor post-shower. The Q-tip and bandage wrapper that didn't quite make it into the trashcan. The pile of magazines stacked next to the toilet (one or two should suffice). You can then dispose of any expired medication or lapsed prescriptions. You can also get rid of anything you got for free from staying at a hotel. You don't need 15 tiny shampoo bottles. With the easy wins out of the way, we can do the work of organizing and simplifying as we go. Let's start with the counters and medicine cabinet.

This is where "like with like" will come in handy. You have products for your teeth (toothbrush, toothpaste, floss, mouth wash). Products for your hair (brushes, combs, hair clips, hair ties, bobby pins, hair rollers, hairspray, gel). Electronics like hair dryers, straighteners, curling irons and electric razors. First-aid items like bandages, alcohol swabs, and a thermometer. Your future self will thank you for knowing where all the first-aid items are. Struggling to find a bandage is the last thing you want to do when you are bleeding all over the place. Maybe there are loose earrings or other jewelry that you can bring together. For grooming there are trimmers, razors, shaving cream, and after shave. There are sticks of deodorant, perfumes, body sprays, and colognes. Don't get me started on all the different types of makeup . . .

After grouping things "like with like, it is time to do the work of discerning what adds value to your life, and what gets in the way. Are there things that you haven't used in months? Probably remove these. When it comes to makeup, ask yourself, "Who am I trying to impress?" Do you wear the makeup you do because you like how it looks, or do you think you need it to be accepted by others? I'm not saying you shouldn't wear makeup, rather I want you to wear it for the right reasons. Not because culture and advertising say you need it to be beautiful. I suggest removing half of your makeup and storing it out of sight for a certain amount of time, maybe a month. You can then experiment with how it feels wearing less makeup and how it feels getting ready without taking the time to decide/find the right makeup for the day. If you miss the other makeup, reintroduce it. If you don't notice, let it go.

For storing your things, clear drawer organizers are a game changer. It ensures that all of your things are contained in the drawer and separated from your other items. Imagine a world where you don't have to scrounge around the drawer to find what you are looking for. Rather, you pull open the drawer and see right away the item you need. These also help keep our spaces clutter-free because you will always know where your things go when you are done using them. Remember, everything has its proper place! Check out thehomeedit.com for ideas and inspiration to transform your bathroom space.

You can then move to the shower. How many bottles do you see? Are you still holding on to the shampoo that is mostly empty, but you can get a little more out of it if you mix it with water? How long has that been going on? Can you simplify it to three items (shampoo, conditioner, and body wash)? What if you just had one 3-1 bottle or one natural all-purpose soap? If that is too ambitious, start by removing the items that you don't use or don't enjoy. Even removing one item is a step towards a decluttered space. Less items in the shower means fewer things to buy (saving you money), and fewer things to knock over (saving you frustration).

Now that you are out of the shower, you need a towel to dry off. How many towels is enough for you? What if each person in the household had two towels each? Then maybe keep a couple extra for when guests come over. Towels that are ripped, frayed, don't hold moisture very well anymore, or are too small to wrap around your body are excellent candidates to get rid of first.

With your bathroom simplified you are able to start and end your day in a stress-free environment. No more scrambling to find the right item as you struggle to leave for work on time. No more frustrations about having hundreds of hair-ties but no idea where they are. Stress and anger are the last things you want to feel before bed or before leaving the house. A clutter-free bathroom is a vital component of your bedtime routine

CHAPTER 8:
HOME OFFICE / DESK RESET:
CLEAR SPACE, CLEAR MIND

Our desks are often the most cluttered spaces in our homes — not because we're lazy, but because they become the "catch-all" for everything: unpaid bills, random sticky notes, half-empty coffee mugs, and chargers we can't quite identify. If your desk looks like a mini storage unit, you're not alone. The good news? A desk reset is one of the fastest ways to boost your productivity and mental clarity.

STEP 1: THE FIVE-MINUTE SWEEP

Set a timer for five minutes. Remove anything that isn't directly related to your work — empty cups, wrappers, yesterday's mail. Just getting the surface clear instantly gives you room to breathe.

STEP 2: CREATE A COMMAND CENTER

Decide where each category of item will live. For example:

- **Incoming papers** → one tray or folder
- **To-do items** → a single notebook or app
- **Supplies** → a drawer organizer for pens, clips, sticky notes

The trick is to have one clear "home" for everything so it doesn't scatter.

STEP 3: LIMIT WHAT LIVES ON YOUR DESK

Keep only your computer, a lamp, and maybe one or two personal items that inspire you (like a plant or photo). Anything more, and your brain reads it as "unfinished work."

STEP 4: END-OF-DAY RESET

Before you shut down each day, take two minutes to straighten your desk. Close your laptop, stack your notebook, and put pens back. Future-you will thank you when you sit down to a clean slate in the morning.

Quick Win: A tidy desk doesn't just look good — it lowers stress and helps your brain shift into "focus mode" faster.

PART III: ADVANCED DECLUTTERING STRATEGIES

You have made it through four major rooms of your house! You should feel so proud. Hopefully it is becoming easier to discern what is important to you, and easier to let go of the things that aren't. Decluttering is like any muscle. It takes practice and repetitions. As a muscle gets stronger, lifting weights becomes easier. In the same way, as we become more skilled in the art of letting go, you will find yourself happily living without things you never thought possible. You now have the tools to deal with other areas of your home such as the entryway, office, or dining room. Maybe you are feeling ambitious and feel ready to tackle projects like the storage room, garage, or attic.

With the big rooms out of the way, we will take a deeper look dealing with paper and digital clutter. Paper and digital clutter affect us both at home, at work, and as we travel. Many people have purses, wallets, and backpacks that perpetually overflow with papers. In this day and age, there is no escaping technology. In order to live an intentional life, we will need to master technology before we are mastered by it. We will conclude Part 3 by discussing storage strategies for staying clutter-free for good.

PAPER CLUTTER SOLUTIONS THAT ACTUALLY STICK

Paper clutter is difficult to keep under control partly because of its diversity. There are receipts and birth certificates. Love notes and notes from a lecture. Bills and children's artwork. Some papers are trash and some are treasures. In this chapter we will discuss ways to tackle paper clutter for good.

Before we can deal with paper clutter, we must first discern what it is. There are four main categories of what paper can be: actionable, informational, sentimental, and recyclable. These categories are not mutually exclusive, and in order to live clutter free, the majority will end up being recyclable. Let's explore these more.

ACTIONABLE

As the name indicates, a piece of paper is actionable if it requires you to take action. It could be a bill to pay, a new credit card to activate, a permission slip to sign, or an invitation to put on your calendar. Let's say that you got a letter from your alma mater asking you to make a donation. You have to decide whether or not you will donate. If not, recycle the document immediately. If yes, make the donation on the spot, then immediately recycle the letter. However, life isn't always that simple. Maybe you need to wait to donate until you get paid. Maybe you need to discuss with your spouse to see if you both want to donate. Maybe you need to decide between other causes to financially support. There are plenty of legitimate reasons why you might hold on to that letter for longer, but the reality is that the longer you wait, the more clutter will accumulate. If the action step isn't clear, schedule a time when you will deal with it.

One tip is to have a designated location for actionable items (remember, everything needs a place), and a scheduled time when you will deal with them. Maybe you schedule time Saturday morning when you go through all the actionable papers. That way you don't have to think about the item throughout the week. You will simply know that everything will be taken care of at the scheduled time. Having a consistent time in which you take action on papers will keep papers from accumulating and robbing you of precious mental energy.

These categories break down a little bit with coupons that you receive in the mail. They contain information ("$5 OFF!!") and require an action (take the coupon to the store to get $5 off). If it is a coupon for a store you don't enjoy, you can recycle. If it is something that you want to use, make a plan to use it before the expiration date.

INFORMATIONAL

True to its name, informational papers are meant to provide you with information. It could be longform information like a newspaper or magazine. It could be as short as a receipt from the grocery store. It could be notes you took from a conference or an explanation of benefits document you received from the doctor. Maybe it is the piece of scratch paper on which you jotted notes when you were on the phone with a client. Two questions to ask when dealing with informational papers are: Is this information relevant? and if yes, for how long do I need this information?

If you know you won't need the information in the future, recycle it. If the information is relevant to you, you must differentiate between what is needed for the long-term versus the short-term. Long-term items would be things like birth certificates, diplomas, and certain legal or tax documents. Short-term informational items are things like the flyer for the upcoming event or a memo from work about a change in company policy.

For the long-term items, file them away in a system that makes sense. For the short-term, consider what you can digitize. Maybe you don't need to hold on to the physical copy of your insurance policy because all of that information is on the app. Anything that you can access online or with a phone call can be recycled. If you like taking notes by hand, consider if there are ways you can convert them into a digital format that is easier to organize, search, and share.

Decluttering informational papers will confront fears of being unprepared or uninformed. "What if I need this in the future?" "Mabe I'll hang on to this just in case . . ." As you get rid of more informational items, you will become more confident that you already have enough information to make the right choice. You will come to find that you need a lot less than you think.

SENTIMENTAL

Sentimental items are some of the toughest to deal with, which is why you should take care of these last. Getting rid of anything that a loved one gave you can feel disrespectful. Sentimental items can be Christmas cards, thank-you notes, love letters, children's artwork, or used up journals (these can also fall in the informational category). You physically can't put every picture your child brings home on the refrigerator. How then do you decide what to keep and what to recycle?

There is not a one size fits all rule, but here are some guidelines. As you go through the different sentimental items, consider which ones still cause you to have a strong emotional reaction. Maybe there was a note of encouragement from a mentor, a letter from a parent apologizing for mistakes they made, a silly card from a college friend that still makes you laugh, or the copy of your wedding vows. Keep the ones that incite a strong positive emotion. After noticing which items cause a strong reaction, it is easier to let go of the ones that you don't feel strongly about.

Another tip is to limit yourself to one box. Knowing exactly how much space you have for sentimental items brings clarity to how much you can keep. The box should remain accessible. So many people have boxes full of papers that go unopened for years and years. If they are going to take up precious space in your home, you should get use out of them. What is the point of hanging on to these meaningful items if you never experience them?

While decluttering sentimental items can be emotionally challenging, it can also be a time to honor memories. Maybe you take one last look at the short story you wrote in grade school, have a laugh, and recycle it with a sense of gratitude for those who helped you grow from that small child to the person you are today. Maybe you take some of the notes you wrote your partner early in your relationship and organize them into a scrapbook as an anniversary gift. Remember, the memories exist outside of the physical paper.

RECYCLABLE

There isn't much to say about this category. Anything that you will never use or are finished using should find its way to the recycling bin. In order to cut down on clutter from mail, one trick is to immediately recycle envelopes. In doing so the letters they contain will be easily accessible. It is also wise to shred anything that has personal information that you wouldn't want others to see. If you decide to purchase a shredder, incorporate shredding into your scheduled time of dealing with actionable papers. If you don't want to buy a shredder, have a designated box or bag to put documents you need shred. Then when it is full, take it to a place locally that offers shredding services.

As your decluttering muscles get stronger, you will become more merciless with the things that find their way into the recycling bin. You will realize that those "just in case" moments are so rare that they actually aren't worth saving paper for. And if those moments do come and you are less prepared than you would like to be, you will see that you are capable enough to handle it.

QUICK TIPS TO PREVENT PAPER CLUTTER

Go paperless for any bill payment or subscription renewal. Most people pay their bills online anyway, so receiving an email notification with the payment link is more efficient than receiving a letter in the mail.

Unsubscribe or opt out from receiving promotional material in the mail. Do you really need those fast food coupons showing up at your house every month? A company like DeleteME is a helpful resource to protect your information so advertisers can't bombard your house with advertisements through the mail.

Digitize what you can. This can be a great way to keep informational and sentimental items without them taking up space. You can scan old pictures and documents and save them on your computer rather than them taking up space in your home. It is often easier to organize digital items than physical items anyway.

You might be asking, "If I digitize all these things, won't that just add to the digital clutter?"

Great question! Because dealing with digital clutter is the topic of the next chapter.

CHAPTER 9: DIGITAL DECLUTTERING: FREE YOUR DEVICES, FREE YOUR MIND

Digital devices might not come to mind for you when you think about decluttering. After all, they aren't taking up physical space. However, that is what makes digital clutter so insidious. Because electronics aren't bound by physical space, you have access to almost infinite information at your fingertips. The overabundance of choices can lead to increased stress and anxiety. Our screens often mirror the clutter that accumulates in our physical spaces. A myriad of files, emails, apps, and social media notifications can feel overwhelming. Digital clutter interrupts productivity and clouds our mental focus. Recognizing digital clutter is the first step to reclaiming both our sanity and efficiency. In this chapter we will discuss some of the major culprits: computer desktops, emails, social media, smart phones, and TV.

COMPUTER DESKTOPS

Picture your computer desktop: a mosaic of icons, each one screaming for attention. That's digital clutter. It might be unnecessary files or PDF downloads you promised you'd sort through but never did. These superfluous elements aren't just hogging storage, they're zapping your concentration. Where do we begin digital tidying?

Start by identifying files that serve no immediate purpose. Things like old drafts, duplicates, and attachments can be deleted. Then organize what remains into clearly labeled folders based on function or project (remember to place like with like). Doing so will streamline access, creating a more efficient virtual workspace. And remember, regularly purging these non-essentials is a habit worth cultivating (Waite, 2024).

EMAILS

Now, let's dive into the murky waters of email management. I want you to know that it is possible to get your email inbox to zero everyday. Apply filters to categorize incoming emails automatically, directing important messages where they belong and sending promotional offers straight to the abyss (Gmail usually does this automatically). Set aside time weekly to unsubscribe from newsletters that add no value to your life. Matt Perman has a helpful resource for getting your inbox to zero. He provides three rules for processing emails: Process items in order from top to bottom, process them one at a time, and never put anything back in your inbox.

Two questions to ask with each email are: "What is this?" and "What is the next action step?" Similar to the chapter on paper clutter, there are four basic types of emails:

1. Emails requiring no action- Delete these right away.
2. Emails requiring actions that take less than two minutes- For a short task, complete it right away and then delete, or move to the "reference" folder.
3. Emails requiring actions that take longer than two minutes- Move to the "reply later" folder.
4. Emails containing information you need- Add to the "reference" folder.

Use folders or labels to group emails by action needed, such as "urgent," "reply later," or "reference." This simple act clarifies priorities and reduces the cognitive load every time you open your inbox (Meyer & Balasco, 2021). Remember, a less cluttered inbox isn't just about reducing stress; it's about enhancing focus. With emails off of your mind, you'll have more mental bandwidth to focus on your most important work.

SOCIAL MEDIA.

For many, social media is the notorious black hole of procrastination. There is also a correlation between high social media use and mental health problems. Social media provides a quick dopamine hit when we are feeling bored or anxious. It's tempting to scroll our problems away, especially when algorithms know exactly how to lure us. Consider, is social media improving your life, or keeping you from living your best life? Remember, social media companies make their money by selling your information to advertisers. The more you scroll, the more you will be tempted to go along with the consumeristic mindset that led to your life being cluttered in the first place.

Maybe your step to declutter social media is to delete your accounts. Maybe your step is to delete the apps from your phone and only check social media while using a computer. Maybe you need to experiment with an app timer. You must ask yourself, "How much social media use is too much? At what point is it keeping me from the most important things?" These practices not only foster healthier digital habits but also provide clearer mental space, allowing for more intentional interactions. Consider employing tools that track your app usage and gently remind you when it's time to step back into the real world.

Social media isn't all bad. It can be very useful for promoting your business, making connections, and keeping up to date on news. You can also curate your feeds to transform social media from a stressor into a source of inspiration and connection. Unfollow accounts that inundate you with negativity or information overload. Fill your feed with content that aligns with your goals and interests, creating a positive online environment. The opposite of clutter is intentionality. Your relationship with social media will improve when you use it intentionally rather than instinctively. By intentional, I mean that you use social media with a specific purpose in mind. By instinctive, I mean getting on social media looking for nothing in particular just to fill the time.

SMART PHONES

Another source of digital chaos is our beloved smartphones. They're marvels of modern technology, yet their constant buzzing can leave you frazzled. Smartphones are both a great help and hindrance to productivity and connectivity. With your smartphone you can call a client, look up a meeting place, and put it on your calendar while the conversation is still happening. However, a phone notification can derail work flow and can take several minutes to regain focus. Similarly, so many face-to-face conversations are ruined when one party checks their phone instead of actively listening. Smartphones are a great tool, but we need to be smart with our smartphones. Here are some tips to reign in smartphone usage.

Similar to social media, discern for yourself how much screen time is too much for you. To get a baseline, check what your average screen time is and consider how you feel about it. You can then start the decluttering process by reviewing which apps you use and which ones you no longer need. Consider deleting social media and email apps. When you are at home, you don't want to be thinking about work emails. You also don't want to see the red number of unread emails every time you unlock your phone. Think of emails as a task to accomplish rather than a newsfeed to frequently check. For the remaining apps, group the essential ones together, while deleting seldom-used apps or tucking them away in folders not on your home screen.

Pictures and videos are another area to declutter. Delete anything that is blurry or unappealing. If you took multiple shots, delete all but the best. Do you really need 17 versions of the same photo? Start by deleting 100 photos. Removing photos you no longer need makes it easier to find the photos you love showing others. You can also consider organizing the pictures based on theme, place, or time period to make finding specific pictures simpler.

Finally, review notifications settings, silencing or limiting those that distract more than delight (Waite, 2024). I recommend turning off notifications for everything except phone calls and text messages. Also, utilize "do not disturb" mode when it is time to focus. As mentioned in the bedroom chapter, consider keeping your phone out of your bedroom when you go to sleep, or put it on airplane mode. This will make it easier to fall asleep and to wake up more intentionally.

TELEVISION

In 2020, Netflix had 36,000 hours of content on their platform, and it is growing each day. If someone watched 8 hours of television per day, it would take more than 12 years to watch everything on Netflix. And their library is constantly expanding. But it isn't just Netflix. There is Amazon Prime, HBO, Disney+, Hulu, Peacock, Paramount+, ESPN, and YoutubeTV. Not to mention all the channels you have with cable or satellite. There is more content than you could ever watch in your lifetime. Paradoxically, too many choices leads to an increase in anxiety. You end up spending your evening looking for something to watch rather than enjoying a movie or show. Having all of the steaming services will also cost you between $100-200 per month, and this is money that you could put towards activities and projects that are more meaningful to you.

Limit your steaming services to a couple at a time. That will save you money (less services to pay for), time (less time searching for something to watch), and mental energy (fewer choices to consider). You can rotate every few months, timing it around when your favorite shows get released.

As you go along your decluttering journey, you learn what helps you live the life you want and what gets in the way. You are the only one who can answer how much TV is right for you, but my hunch is that it is less than you think. For one week, name a specific time limit for TV time. Maybe it is 3 hours, maybe it's 15. Then schedule TV time on your calendar. Setting time limits help you curate for quality. If you know you can only watch one thing on a particular night, you will be more likely to choose something that is high-quality rather than trash TV (however you define it).

Ultimately, conquering digital clutter demands commitment—a dedication to continuous evaluation and maintenance. Think of it as digital gardening: uprooting weeds, nurturing valuable plants, and enjoying the fruits of your labor. By doing so, you create a digital ecosystem that's not only organized but also conducive to growth, both personally and professionally. The best things in life are experienced in the physical world. Go "touch grass" and re-experience the simple joys this world has to offer.

CHAPTER 10: STORAGE THAT WORKS: ORGANIZING WITHOUT OVERSTUFFING

There is a reason that the chapter on storage and organization is near the end of the book. It is a mistake to organize without first minimizing. I hope you recall that for every area of the house we first discussed removing items (Purging is the first letter in PLACE, after all). It is important to first do the work of purging unused and unwanted items before organizing. Otherwise, you won't be clutter-free, you will just have well organized clutter. When you have fewer items, organizing becomes easier. You have done the work of simplifying, now what do you do with the stuff you decide to keep? We will go deeper into the principles of "like with like" and "accessibility." We will also discuss unique storage options which are especially helpful in small spaces.

LIKE WITH LIKE

Two guiding principles for this book are that everything has a place and everything has a purpose. I'll take it a step further to say that the places in which we put our items should serve the purposes of a particular space. For example, where you store things in the kitchen should result in an easier cooking experience. Where you store things in the bathroom should make it easy to get ready in the morning. One way to ensure this happens is to keep similar items together. Your goal should be to never ask the question, "Now, where did I put that . . .?"

ACCESSIBLE

You have gained clarity on how to group your possessions, now we'll consider effective ways to store them. For your sanity, you want the things you use frequently to be easily accessible. For example, you might place your razor in a different location if you shave once a day rather than once a month.

An important element of accessibility is visibility. Here are some tips to ensure visibility:

- Use small boxes to keep things separate in drawers.

    ○ This is especially helpful with bathroom drawers, nightstands, and drawers that contain a variety of small items.

- Use clear storage containers.

    ○ You don't want to open multiple containers to find what you are looking for. Clear containers (preferably labeled) are a game-changer in the pantry, fridge, and office because you can see what is in them without opening them.

- Stack things vertically instead of horizontally.

    ○ Marie Kondo advocates for putting shirts in a drawer vertically so that you can see all of your options when getting dressed. When shirts are stacked on top of each other, you have to sort through many of them to find the one you want. This holds true for things like books and papers too.

- Place bulk items out of sight until you need them.

    ○ You don't need five tubes of toothpaste in the drawer at the same time. Keep one in the drawer and store the rest in a closet or a different location that makes sense.

- Invest in cabinets that have pull-out drawers.

- If you keep pots and pans on the bottom shelves in your kitchen, it is often difficult to find what you are looking for. Having drawers that pull out will make it easier to access.

- Spaciousness is your friend

  - Spaces that are overflowing with items make it difficult to find what you are looking for. Imagine a closet in which you can clearly see every outfit that you own. What if you were able to leave 3-5 inches of space between each clothing item hanging in your closet? How might that change how you feel about getting dressed?

CREATIVE STORAGE SOLUTIONS FOR SMALL SPACES

Some of you reading this might live in a dorm room, small apartment, or maybe you are considering a transition into a tiny home. If that is true for you, here are some ways to maximize storage in your minimal space.

UTILIZING VERTICAL STORAGE SOLUTIONS

Wall-mounted shelves are a classic yet transformative solution. These versatile structures not only reclaim floor space but also serve as functional art pieces. Imagine walking into your living room, where sleek floating shelves host vibrant succulents, a few well-placed books, and framed photos capturing cherished memories. Beyond their practical use, such shelves invite creativity. Paint them bold colors or choose minimalist designs that blend seamlessly with your walls. Wall-mounted shelves allow you to express personality while keeping clutter at bay. With a touch of DIY spirit, you can customize the shelf arrangements to suit any room's purpose.

Over-the-door organizers are another great solution. Quick to install, these adaptable tools are ideal for every room from bathrooms to kitchens. Imagine a busy morning where all your essentials are neatly lined up within arm's reach. In the bathroom, use an over-the-door organizer to hold toiletries, hair tools, or even rolled-up towels. Meanwhile, in the kitchen, it can cleverly store spices, snacks, or cleaning supplies, liberating valuable cabinet space. When choosing an organizer, look for sturdy materials and adjustable shelves to match various needs.

Diving deeper into sophisticated storage, consider hanging basket systems. These beauties are perfect for those who want function with flair. They create dynamic storage that's easy to adapt based on seasons or usage. For instance, in the spring, fill them with potpourri and blooming flowers; in the winter, swap out for gloves and scarves. These baskets add texture and depth to a space, transforming utility into décor. Additionally, using them allows for quick clean-ups; simply toss in the odds and ends that accumulate throughout the day. Their charm lies in both practicality and artistry.

Lastly, let's not overlook the adaptability of ladder shelves. While not a strictly vertical fixture like the others, ladder shelves offer a unique twist on traditional shelving. Leaning against a wall, they provide a movable and creative solution for displaying items. As a young adult or college student, you might find them perfect for holding textbooks, plants, or even storing kitchen essentials if you're short on cabinets. The flexibility they offer to reorganize quickly means they can evolve with your needs, making them a fantastic investment for ever-changing environments.

Embracing these vertical storage solutions isn't just about making do with limited square footage; it's about reimagining those limitations as opportunities. Whether you're setting up your first apartment or refining your home office, these options cater to enhancing both functionality and aesthetics in your space.

MULTI-PURPOSE FURNITURE TIPS

First up is the storage ottoman. At first glance, it seems to be just a stylish footrest or extra seat, but lift the lid, and you will find a nifty storage compartment. These ottomans are perfect for tucking away those pesky items that seem to have no home (remote controls, magazines, or even extra blankets). With a variety of designs available, from plush velvet to sleek leather, they add a touch of elegance to any room while keeping clutter cleverly out of sight.

Next on the list are foldable tables. Whether you need a dining area for a romantic dinner, a workspace for an impromptu project, or simply a spot to relax with a cup of tea, foldable tables adapt to your needs at a moment's notice. When not in use, these tables can be easily stored away, freeing up valuable floor space. Perfect for young adults and college students who need their homes to work as hard as they do, foldable tables transform living rooms into functional multipurpose areas without sacrificing style.

The Murphy bed is ideal for anyone challenged with turning a single room into multiple living spaces. By folding into the wall during the day, a Murphy bed allows a bedroom to morph into a home office, yoga studio, or entertainment area. These beds epitomize the concept of transforming space, offering a practical solution for maximizing small bedrooms.

Convertible sofas are another masterpiece in the world of multifunctional furniture. These clever designs effortlessly transition from a stylish couch to a comfortable bed, ensuring you're always ready for surprise overnight guests. Unlike traditional sleeper sofas that compromise on comfort, modern convertibles often come with memory foam mattresses or high-quality padding. This ensures that neither form nor function is sacrificed, allowing the furniture to blend seamlessly into your decor while adding significant sleeping space.

What makes multifunctional furniture truly special is its ability to simplify life by removing unnecessary distractions. For example, choosing a convertible sofa means no more wrestling with inflatable mattresses or stacking futons; it's an elegant all-in-one solution. Storage ottomans eliminate the need for additional bulky storage units, which might otherwise clutter your living space. A foldable table negates the necessity of separate dining and work tables. These furniture pieces illustrate that, sometimes, less really is more.

CREATING HIDDEN STORAGE AREAS

Under-bed storage is another fantastic strategy, especially in smaller spaces where every square foot counts. Using this space efficiently can help keep seasonal items like winter coats or extra bedding out of sight but still within reach when needed. By reducing visual clutter, under-bed storage helps maintain a clean and spacious feel in the room without sacrificing storage capacity.

For some, staircase storage might be a unique yet highly effective solution. Many homes have staircases with untapped potential beneath them. With some creativity, this typically wasted space can morph into an array of storage compartments. Imagine sliding drawers or pull-out shelves neatly tucked away under each step, ideal for shoes, books, or even pantry items. This smart use of space not only helps keep things organized but also adds a touch of intrigue to your home's design. Tailoring these compartments to your specific needs can lead to an individually customized solution that serves practical purposes beautifully (Bern, 2020).

Furniture with hidden compartments is another brilliant strategy for maintaining a clutter-free environment. Picture a coffee table that lifts open to reveal storage for remote controls, magazines, or even blankets. These pieces serve dual functions— providing comfort and style while discreetly concealing everyday items. By integrating such multifunctional furniture, you can streamline your living space and keep frequently used items at hand without having them out on display.

The goal of this chapter was to give you ideas for how to cultivate a space that is both functional and beautiful. Assuming you aren't selling all of your possessions to live as a monk, you will always have possessions to properly store. Keeping them contained, organized, and in a location that makes sense is essential to life a clutter-free life. Your home should be a space of peace and tranquility. There are enough things in life that stress you out. Don't let your home be another!

PART V: KEEPING IT CLUTTER- FREE FOR GOOD

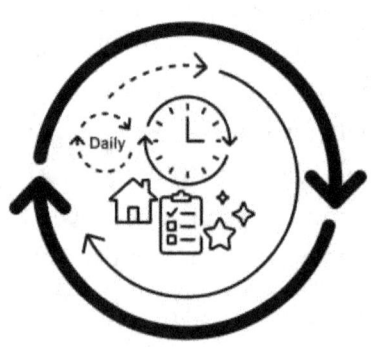

DAILY, WEEKLY, AND QUARTERLY TIPS

If you have been decluttering and organizing as you read this book, congratulations on your tidy and organized home! However, decluttering is a journey, not a destination. Maintaining a clutter-free home requires intentionality and diligence. If we aren't mindful, clutter will accumulate and creep up on us without us realizing.

In order to keep the chaos at bay, we need habits and rhythms to consistently help us live clutter-free. These habits should require little effort, little time, and little thought to accomplish. Habits that are quick, easy, and obvious tend to last longer than big dramatic goals. In the following chapters we will explore a mindset shift that will impact almost every aspect of clutter-free living (Ch. 11). We will then discuss habits for removing clutter daily (Ch. 12), weekly (Ch. 13), and quarterly (Ch. 14)

CHAPTER 11:
THE "ONE-TOUCH" RULE FOR STAYING CLUTTER-FREE

The "One-Touch" rule is a simple habit that, if you stick with it, will make it so much easier to keep clutter at bay. Remember the principle that everything has a place, and clutter occurs when things are out of place. The "One-Touch" rule, true to its name, encourages you to immediately put things in their proper place after using it, thus, only touching an item one time.

Think about what you do when you get home from work. Maybe you kick your shoes off at the door, throw your keys and the mail on the kitchen counter, drape your coat over a chair, and leave your work clothes on the floor as you slip into something more comfortable. As you mindlessly do what you have done thousands of times before, you left things out of place. Your home will remain cluttered until you go back and move all the items a second time to put them away.

Here is how your homecoming routine would look if you followed the One-Touch rule. You would get home, take off your shoes and put them on the shoe rack (or wherever you put your shoes), hang up your coat on the hook by the door, set your keys in the bowl or on the key hook, open the mail and sort it into its appropriate category (recycle, actionable, informational, sentimental), and put your clothes in the hamper (or hang them if they are still wearable).

None of the above tasks are difficult. They all take less than a minute to accomplish. So, why is it so hard to consistently put things in their place right away? Odds are you do what you do because it is what you've always done. As we discussed above, our brains love routine. They love to go on auto-pilot in order to free up mental space to focus on other things. However, it is important to admit when a habit hinders us instead of helps us.

In order to get started with the One-Touch rule, think about where your pain points are. Maybe it is leaving dishes on the table. Maybe it is clothes on the floor. Maybe you always struggle to find your keys. Maybe it is leaving empty bottles and cans on the counter. Start where you will most feel the effects, and start with one thing at a time.

How can you design your environment to make putting things back in their place the obvious option? Let's use the clothes on the floor as our example. How is your environment setting you up to fail? Maybe your laundry basket is in an inconvenient location. Maybe your laundry basket is already full of clothes. After identifying the road blocks, structure your space to get the results you want.

The next step is to name your habit. "After I take my shirt off I will immediately put it in the basket." You can then give yourself a high five to celebrate taking the first step in conquering clothes clutter. When you get to the point where you stop leaving clothes on the floor without thinking about it, you can now add another habit. Let's talk about dishes!

In terms of the clutter-free hierarchy, putting dishes in the dishwasher (if available) is better than in the sink and the sink is better than the table or counter. Putting dishes in the dishwasher means only touching the dish once white the sink requires two touches. As you recall from chapter 4, we want to limit the time that it takes for the dishes to be washed, dried, and put away. Not leaving clean dishes in the dishwasher for too long will enable you to practice the One-Touch rule with dishes more consistently.

Other areas to follow the One-Touch rule would be throwing trash away immediately, putting books on the shelf when you are done reading them, putting leftovers in a container

As you handle things in your home, remember this rule: "Don't put it down, put it away." The more you can do that, the easier it will be to experience the calm that comes from a clutter-free environment.

CHAPTER 12:
15-MINUTE DAILY HABITS THAT PREVENT PILE-UPS

An important truth to keep in mind is that something is always better than nothing. Author James Clear once said, "Two is twice as good as one, but one is infinitely better than zero." The small decluttering habits we do everyday are bricks we are laying to build the road to calm and peace.

I'm assuming you are utilizing the One-Touch rule that we discussed in the previous chapter, so I will try not to be redundant. Here is a strategy for utilizing five-minute chunks of time three times per day. Once in the morning, once in the evening, and once before winding down for bed.

MORNING

As you think about your morning routine, consider, "Where does it make the most sense to include five minutes of decluttering?" For me, it is while I wait for my coffee to brew. Maybe for you it makes more sense to declutter after breakfast, after exercising, or meditating. The most important thing is that it is a task you already do everyday. Adding two new habits at once usually isn't sustainable.

After you complete your established habit, set a timer for five minutes, or play find an upbeat music playlist (two songs should be enough). Introducing a timer can dramatically alter the dynamics of decluttering, converting it from a laborious duty into a stimulating activity. By setting a timer for five minutes, you fabricate a sense of urgency and concentration, compelling you to dedicate undivided attention to the task at hand. Introducing music adds an element of joy and play. There is a reason why

Snow White and her dwarf friends whistle while they work. Music adds a lightness to what could otherwise be drudgery.

Now you are ready to tackle your target area. Maybe you have dishes to do, counters to clear, or floors to sweep. If you meditate in your living room, it would make the most sense to pick up things in the living room: books, magazines, clothes, pillows, electronics, toys, etc. If your launching habit is brushing your teeth, you can straighten the counters, organize the medicine chest, or pick up clothes or towels that fell on the floor.

Five minutes might not be enough time to finish everything you want, but it is a great place to start. You will begin noticing that your space looks 5% better than it did before, and those micro-wins will fuel you to stick with the decluttering process.

EVENING

Let's say you get home from work, do an activity or home project, and now it's time for dinner. Before or after dinner is a great anchor habit for decluttering. A lot of cooking is waiting. Waiting for water to boil, waiting for things in the oven to preheat, waiting for dinner to bake, waiting for things to be cool enough to eat. Times of waiting are great opportunities to declutter. Maybe you start washing the dishes you just used to prepare the meal, or begin sorting mail into appropriate categories, or wipe down the counters before the tomato sauce hardens. Incorporating decluttering into the process of cooking is a great way to redeem down time.

Setting a timer or music to declutter after dinner also works well. After you finish eating, you have to pick up your dishes anyway. Adding a couple more minutes won't feel too difficult. Also, if you eat with others you get the benefit of a team. Two people working for five minutes is the same as one person working for ten minutes. Maybe one of you does the dishes while another cleans the table and takes out the trash.

There is always work involved with dinner. Even when you order takeout there are wrappers and bags to clear away. Associating a five-minute decluttering habit with dinner makes sense because you are already doing work. Oftentimes starting is the hardest part. It is easier to continue a task than begin anew.

BEFORE WINDING DOWN

As the end of day approaches, hopefully you have established an intentional bedtime routine that allows you to relax at the end of the day. Maybe you read, enjoy a cup of tea, do a jigsaw puzzle, or watch a show. Whatever it is, try incorporating one more five-minute decluttering session before you wind down for bed.

What would be most helpful to have completed so you don't have to deal with it in the morning? Maybe it is a stack of papers. Maybe there is laundry that needs to be folded. Maybe the trash and recycling are overflowing. Your future self will thank you when they don't have to deal with the problem area in the morning. An added bonus is that after you complete your five-minute task you can reward yourself with an activity that you enjoy. And how much sweeter will it be when you have the feeling of accomplishment instead of the feeling of guilt and anxiety?

Fifteen minutes is 1% of your day. Being intentional to consistently declutter for 1% of your time is worth it to maintain a calm and clutter-free environment. Incorporate these habits into your daily rhythm and see the power a 1% change can make!

CHAPTER 13:
THE WEEKEND MINI-RESET: REFRESH YOUR HOME IN UNDER AN HOUR

Every Friday afternoon Jews around the world prepare for Shabbat. Shabbat is the highlight or pinnacle of the week. It is a day that is set apart from the rest of the week. Shabbat is a holy day. It is a day when they dress up, break out the fine China and silver, and stop all of their work. Rabbi Aryeh Kaplan taught, "Anticipate [Shabbat] as you would an important visitor. After all, Shabbat is the Queen of all Creation . . . Clean up your room and tidy your belongings. Put away all weekday things. Prepare your surroundings to reflect the Shabbat mood." (*Erev Shabbat: Transitioning into Shabbat*, 2006)

Shabbat officially begins at sunset on Friday night. Candles are lit, prayers are said, and food is shared between loved ones. Shabbat is an intentional rhythm of rest and celebration that occurs every seven days for the Jewish people. Shabbat is a day to reset spiritually, mentally, emotionally, and physically. It is also a day to reset your living space.

While I am not Jewish, I believe we can all learn from their Shabbat practices. Shabbat places a hard boundary for work. No work is to be done on Shabbat. If you knew there was one day each week when you didn't allow yourself to work, how might that transform your work week? Maybe you would be more focused, knowing that there is a hard deadline to complete the tasks. Maybe you would be more selective about the projects you take on instead of impulsively saying "Yes" to every request. Hard boundaries are necessary to confront chaos.

Notice how Rabbi Kaplan said to "prepare your surroundings to reflect the Shabbat mood." The Shabbat mood is one of peace, joy, rest, and celebration. Regardless of your religious tradition, I bet the idea of having a living space that reflects the Shabbat mood sounds appealing. It does for me. The focus of this chapter will be on resetting your home each weekend. Imagine starting each week with your home completely set in order. Trash and recycling taken out, all of your clothes folded and put away, dishes washed and put away, and all books on the shelf. Let's explore how to get there.

HIT THE RESET BUTTON

If you have been utilizing the One-touch rule and the 15-minutes of daily decluttering, your weekend reset shouldn't take more than an hour. You have done most of the work already. Start by gathering all of your dirty clothes to start a load of laundry. While the laundry is going, you can turn your attention to a different area of the house. A flow that makes sense is to start in the kitchen, then living room, bedroom, and end with the bathroom (depending on how many loads of laundry you need to do).

In the kitchen, you will need to do the dishes, clear the counters, make sure there is no expired food in the fridge, and clean the floors. As you clear the counters, gather any paper. You will deal with this at the end.

In the living room, you will pick up any toys, electronics, books, magazines, or trash that might be lying about (I'm assuming you already picked up clothes and dishes). When everything is off the floor and put away, you can vacuum the floors. If needed, dust the furniture.

The bedroom should be pretty straightforward. Your clothes are already being washed and dried, so they aren't on the floor. All that you need to do is pick up anything that doesn't belong, make your bed, and fold and put away clothes when the laundry is done. Vacuum and dust as needed.

Finally, the bathroom. The first step is to pick up anything that is on the floor (hopefully you already gathered dirty clothes and towels and put them in the laundry). You can take inventory on the drawers to see if there is anything you need to purchase or get rid of. Next is to clean the sink, toilet, and shower if needed. Sweep the floors and empty the trash can and you are done in that space!

If it took you 15 minutes in these four rooms, your house would be completely reset in an hour (depending on how large your house is and how many rooms you have). You could spend that hour catching up on your favorite podcast to make the time more enjoyable. The last step is to process the papers from the week and take out the trash and recycling. Take action on where it is needed, recycle, shred, or store the rest.

Congratulations! You have officially reset your home. You are ready to host loved ones, or stay in, light some candles and take advantage of the newfound calm. We have considered habits for daily and weekly decluttering. We will conclude with exploring ideas around seasonal decluttering

CHAPTER 14: SEASONAL DECLUTTERING: A FRESH START EVERY FEW MONTHS

The changing of seasons is a great time to declutter and reconsider your space and possessions. Spring cleaning isn't just a cliché. It's a natural motivator as you're already in the mindset of refreshing your space. Similarly, the start of a new academic term or the change of seasons can serve as perfect opportunities to revamp your living area. These events bring an inherent sense of renewal and make the process more engaging. When seasons change, we need to consider shifts in wardrobe, accessories, decor, meals, and activities. Let's explore these more.

In Chapter 6 we discussed Project 333 (33 items of clothing for 3 months). The timing is intentional because the change in the seasons leads to a natural wardrobe shift. Even if you don't participate in Project 333, you will likely change your wardrobe when the seasons change. Maybe you have a Winter wardrobe that you utilize December-February, consisting of jeans, flannels, and heavy sweaters. Your Spring wardrobe (March-May), would have a mix of pants and shorts, long-sleeve t-shirts, and rain jackets. Your Summer wardrobe (June-August) would have more shorts, tank-tops, and short-sleeve shirts. Finally, your Fall wardrobe (September-November) would have a mixture of shorts, pants, shirts, flannels, and hoodies. The changing of seasons is a great time to evaluate which clothes you wear, and which ones you don't. One trick is to turn hangers so that the rounded part of the hook is facing towards the wall. Once you wear the item, place the hanger so that the rounded hook is facing you. At the end of each quarter you will be able to easily tell which items you haven't worn.

Winter coats, hats and gloves, and snow boots give way to rain boots, rain coats, and umbrellas. Rain coats give way to sunscreen, sun glasses, and sandals. Sandals give way to hiking boots and the return of beanies. When the seasons change, adjust your drop off zones to reflect the reality of the season. In the winter, keep hats and gloves accessible and put the sunscreen and beach towels in storage. Take inventory for things that are damaged or went unused. Maybe you get to the end of winter and realize that you only wore three beanies. You should feel empowered to only keep the three hats you wore.

Not everyone changes their decor to match the season, but if you do, it is a great time to take inventory on which items still bring you joy. When we are forced to handle each decoration to put it in storage, you can reflect on how that item makes you feel. It might be the case that your preferences have changed and it is time to say goodbye to that item. It is also a good time to throw away any items that are broken. Also consider if the amount of decorations fits your space, or if it leaves the room feeling cluttered.

Consider how your diet might change with the seasons. Fall might bring more pumpkin and apples while summer brings more watermelon and tomatoes. Fall and winter are also great for soups and stews. In summer we buy popsicles. In winter we buy hot chocolate. Changing of seasons is a good opportunity to evaluate diet and meal planning. Food tends to go to waste when we aren't intentional about what we put in our carts at the grocery store. Maybe you plan on having lighter meals when the weather is warm and heavier meals when the weather is colder.

Finally, activities vary drastically depending on the season. In the summer you might mow your lawn weekly. In the winter, you might snowblow your driveway weekly. You will trade your kayaks for sleds, roller blades for skis. Changing of the seasons is an opportunity to evaluate which activities you genuinely enjoy, and which activities you feel like you should enjoy but don't. For example, maybe you get to winter and realize that you didn't take your kayak out once this year. You might ask yourself,

"How many times did I use it the previous year?" You might come to realize that the kayak doesn't bring you the joy you thought it would. That is okay! You have the freedom to let it go. You can sell it or gift it to a loved one who will get more use out of it. Don't let seasons change without giving careful thought to your possessions. The changing of the season provides four natural opportunities each year to be honest about where you are in life and where you want to go. Don't let it pass you by!

90/90 RULE

The 90/90 Rule is helpful at any time of year, but it is especially useful when seasons change. The 90/90 Rule simply asks, "Have I used this item in the past 90 days? Will I use this item in the next 90 days?" If the answer is "yes" to either question, keep it. If it is "no" to both, get rid of it. There might be exceptions to the rule (a swimsuit in December, perhaps), but there is a good chance that if you aren't using an item for one half of the year, you also aren't using it for the other half.

In this book we have gone room by room removing items that don't serve a purpose and we found a convenient place for everything else. You have learned different rules and habits that enable you to maintain a clutter-free environment with minimal effort. However, these won't mean anything unless they are connected to a deeper purpose in your life. We began this book by examining a clutter-filled life. We will now conclude by examining what is waiting for you on the other side of decluttering.

MOTIVATIONAL VISION EXERCISE

YOUR CLUTTER-FREE LIFE: IMAGINE THE SHIFT

Take a moment, close your eyes, and imagine waking up tomorrow in a clutter-free home. Walk through the scene in your mind:

- You step into the kitchen and see **clear counters** — no dishes piled high, no random gadgets in the way.

- You walk into the living room, where everything has a place. The surfaces are clear, the floor is open, and you can finally sit down without moving piles first.
- You enter your bedroom — it feels like a calm retreat. The bed is clear, the nightstand holds only a lamp and a book you actually enjoy.
- When you open your closet, you see clothes you love, organized in a way that makes getting dressed simple and stress-free.
- At your desk, you find only what you need: your laptop, a notebook, a pen. You feel ready to focus, not distracted.

Now, ask yourself: **How would your day feel different if this was your reality every morning?**

- Would you feel calmer?
- More in control?
- Excited to start the day instead of weighed down?

This vision is within your reach. Every small action you take — one drawer, one corner, one habit at a time — is building toward this life. Whenever you feel stuck or tempted to give up, come back to this picture of your clutter-free life. Let it remind you what you're working toward.

CONCLUSION: LIVING LIGHTER: HOW A CLUTTER-FREE SPACE IMPROVES YOUR LIFE

Your alarm goes off. You open your eyes and you feel well rested and ready to greet the day. Before getting out of bed you take a deep thankful breath. You then get up, make your bed, and go to the kitchen to make your morning coffee. The counters are clear except your journal and a pen so you can note what goals you want to accomplish today. The sink is empty. You just need to unload the dishrack and dishwasher. You do that while you wait for the coffee.

You then sit down at the table with your coffee and a small breakfast as you read that personal development book that has been on your list for far too long. After breakfast, you take your phone off the charger for the first time. You check your calendar to gain some clarity about what you are doing today. You see a couple text messages, but nothing urgent.

It's time to shower. You grab the clean towel from the closet and hop in. You know exactly where everything you need is. You then go to your closet to pick out your clothes for the day. You can see all of your options laid out for you and you love all of your clothes, so getting dressed is hassle-free. You grab your pre-made lunch from the fridge and head to the office. You have plenty of time, so you drive the speed limit and take the scenic route.

You get to your desk, which has your computer, a notepad and pen, and an inbox with your tasks for the day. Files for other projects are stored out of sight. You start working on a key task to move your current project forward. After two hours of deep work, you take a break and check emails. Only 35 Unread. Manageable. You quickly work through what can be deleted, which require an immediate response, which provide information you need to know, and which require you to take action. You process your email inbox to zero in thirty minutes. Now it's time for a staff meeting before lunch with your coworker.

After work, you meet up with a friend to go for a run around the park to take advantage of the nice weather. Winter will be here before you know it. You have plenty of time after the run to catch up on what is happening in each other's lives. You then go home and make a healthy meal of pasta and vegetables. Quick and delicious! Following dinner you wash the dishes and wipe down the table and counters. All clear for the next day. There is even leftover pasta to bring to work the next day. You have a couple of hours before you need to go to bed, so you make some tea and curl up with a fun book. Maybe you give your friend a call. You could use a good laugh or a good cry.

You then start your bedtime routine, put your phone on airplane mode, set your alarm, and get in your made bed. You go to bed tired, but fulfilled, knowing that you spent your time and energy on the things you find meaningful and joyful. You smile as you drift off to sleep because you get to do it all again tomorrow.

After reading this book, I hope you believe that the clutter-free life described above is possible for you. It will look different for you depending on your job, marital status, and stage of life, but the principle of spending your best time and energy on the things that bring joy and meaning to your life still apply.

By doing the work of decluttering, you learn to let go. You can let go of fear and expectations that hold you back. You will have more spaciousness in your budget and calendar. You know that everything in your home serves a purpose and has a designated space. By taking one small step at a time, you can keep a clutter free environment without much mental effort.

The newfound time and mental focus will allow you to dream bigger dreams and pursue new adventures.

Life is not found in an abundance of possessions. In fact, our abundance can keep us from the life we were meant to live. You only get one life. Don't let clutter keep you from living it

BONUS RESOURCES: ROOM-BY-ROOM DECLUTTER CHECKLIST

LIVING ROOM RESET

Your Goal: Create a calm, welcoming space to relax.

15-Minute Flow:

- Grab a basket and do a "sweep" of anything that doesn't belong (mugs, toys, tech, laundry).
- Fold throws, fluff pillows, stack books or magazines neatly.
- Wipe coffee table and remote controls.
- Declutter one drawer or shelf only (not the whole unit).

Quick Hack: Store a stylish basket in the corner for ongoing clutter grabs—what's out of sight is out of stress!

KITCHEN RESET

Your Goal: Make cooking and eating feel easier and less chaotic.

15-Minute Flow:

- Empty the sink. If short on time—stack neatly, soak, or rinse to reduce overwhelm.
- Clear and wipe counters—remove anything that doesn't serve daily use.
- Open one cabinet or drawer—ditch expired spices or random lids.
- Sweep or vacuum the floor.

Quick Hack: Keep a "toss bin" under the sink for quick, regular purging.

BEDROOM RESET

Your Goal: Create a peaceful retreat that invites sleep and calm.

15-Minute Flow:

- Make the bed (yes, it makes the whole room feel cleaner instantly).
- Clear nightstands and dresser tops—leave only essentials.
- Pick up clothes and sort—laundry, rehang, or donate. •\
- Open windows for a 5-minute fresh air flow.

Quick Hack: Store a donation bag inside your closet for ongoing clothing edits.

BATHROOM RESET

Your Goal: Turn chaos into a calm, spa-like zone.

15-Minute Flow: •

- Toss old products, worn towels, or near-empty bottles.
- Wipe down sink, mirror, and counters.
- Organize daily-use items in trays or bins.
- Replace one "blah" item with something calming—like a candle or plant.

Quick Hack: Use over-the-door hooks or vertical storage to maximize space.

YOUR EXCLUSIVE ACCESS

Thank you so much for reading *From Chaos to Calm*. I'm truly grateful for your time and support—it means the world to me!

If you'd like to continue this journey together, I'd love to stay connected. By joining my newsletter, you'll receive uplifting tips, practical insights, and early access to my upcoming books—straight to your inbox.

👉 Sign up here

https://theawesomereaders.com/

Or scan the QR Code below

Until next time,

Amelia Sagewood

REFERENCE LIST

11 Decluttering Motivation Tips: Useful Guide - EZ CleanUp . (2024, July 3). Ezcleanup.com. https:// ezcleanup.com/11-decluttering-motivation-tips/

Ambardekar, N. (2021, March 7). *Slideshow: How Clutter Can Affect Your Health* . WebMD. https:// www.webmd.com/balance/ss/slideshow-clutter- affects-health

Beckwith, A., & Parkhurst, E. (2022, July 1). *The Mental Health Benefits of Decluttering.* Extension.usu.edu. https://extension.usu.edu/ mentalhealth/articles/the-mental-benefits-of- decluttering

Fogg, B. J. (2019). *TINY HABITS : The small changes that change everything.* Houghton Mifflin Harcourt.

Rita's Minimalist Essentials. (2024, November 15). *Staying Motivated to Declutter: 5 Tips to Keep You on Track* . Design Services LTD | https://www.designservicesltd.com/2024/11/15/staying-motivated-to-declutter-5-tips- to-keep-you-on-track/

Sander, L. (2019, January 25). *What does clutter do to your brain and body?* NewsGP. https:// www1.racgp.org.au/newsgp/clinical/what-does-clutter-do-to-your-brain-and-body

Silverthorn, V. (2018, April 18). *Decluttering Strategy* . Oprah.com. https://www.oprah.com/ home/decluttering-strategy

admin. (2024, February 25). *How to Set Clear Decluttering Goals for a Clutter Free Space - Dare to Declutter* . Dare to Declutter. https:// www.daretodeclutter.co.uk/tips/clear-decluttering- goals/

Breaking Free from Procrastination: Actionable Tips with Risa Williams . (2024, August 14). Apple Podcasts. https://podcasts.apple.com/nz/podcast/ breaking-free-from-procrastination-actionable- tips/id1485473251?i=1000665232559

Burger, J. (2023, June 5). *How to Let Go of Sentimental Items While Decluttering* . Simply + Fiercely. https://www.simplyfiercely.com/sentimental-items/

Botman, C. (2021, July 30). *Minimalism and its Positive Effects on your Mental Health / Seasoned Journeys.* https://seasoned-journeys.com/minimalism-and-its-positive-effects-on-your- mental-health/

Downsizing Decluttering. (2024, November 19). *5 Top Secrets to Beat Decision Fatigue with Fewer Choices | Design Services LTD* . Design Services

Erev Shabbat: Transitioning Into Shabbat. (2006, July 17). Orthodox Union. https://www.ou.org/holidays/erev_shabbat_the_eve_of_shabbat/

LTD | Rita Wilkins, the Downsizing Designer, Is a Nationally Recognized Interior Design and Lifestyle Design Expert. Through Her Best-Selling Book, Speaking Engagements, and Design Insight, Rita Has Changed the Lives of Thousands of People throughout the United States. https://www.designservicesltd.com/2024/11/19/5-top-secrets-to-beat-decision-fatigue-with-fewer- choices/

Mills, K. (2023, February). *Speaking of Psychology: Why clutter stresses us out, with Dr. Joseph Ferrari, PhD.* Apa.org. https://www.apa.org/news/podcasts/speaking-of-psychology/clutter

Overcoming Procrastination: Strategies for Beating Productivity Killers . (2024, March 29). Any.do Blog | Productivity Tips & Trends, Delivered. https://www.any.do/blog/overcoming- procrastination-strategies-for-beating-productivity- killers/

R.D, E. P. M. P. H. (2024, April 24). *How to Declutter Sentimental Items* . Modern Minimalism. https://modernminimalism.com/ how-to-declutter-sentimental-items/

Talane Miedaner. (2023, October 11). *Conquer Decision Fatigue with 5 Decluttering Strategies* .

LifeCoach.com. https://www.lifecoach.com/ articles/simplify-clutter/conquer-decision-fatigue- with-5-decluttering-strategies/

Becker, Joshua. (2020, January 27). *How Minimalism Can Help You Find Wellness* . Becoming Minimalist. https://www.becomingminimalist.com/wellness/

Combiths, S. (2020, June 15). *The 27 Greatest Decluttering Tips of All Time* . Apartment Therapy. https://www.apartmenttherapy.com/decluttering-tips-36704986

Gallagher, N. (2016, February 11). *Organize Like a Pro: A 5-Step Process for Organizing Any Space* . Refined Rooms. https://refinedroomsllc.com/a-5-step-process-for-organizing-any-space/

How to Declutter Your Home: A Ridiculously ThoroughGuide (n.d.).

Www.budgetdumpster.com. https://www.budgetdumpster.com/resources/how-to- declutter-your-home.php

How to Organize Your Life . (2024). Beforesunset.ai. https://www.beforesunset.ai/post/ how-to-organize-your-life

Svitlana Popovska. (2024, March 29). *Work Smarter, Not Harder: Practical Steps on How to Be More Organized* . XTiles. https://xtiles.app/en/blog/how-to-be-more-organized/

Simplicity, B. T. (2023, May 30). *Slow Decluttering: The Benefits of Decluttering Slowly* . BALANCE through SIMPLICITY. https://balancethroughsimplicity.com/slow-decluttering/

https://www.facebook.com/TheSavvyCouple. (2024, April 24). *9 Simple Steps For How to Organize Your Life Effectively* . The Savvy Mama. https://thesavvymama.com/how-to-organize-your- life/

https://www.facebook.com/realsimple. (2024). *The Micro-Decluttering Method Could Help You Finally Tidy Up Your Space and Keep It That Way*

. Real Simple. https://www.realsimple.com/micro- decluttering-8662555

5 Minimalist Tips for Clutter-Free Bathroom Storage . (2023, July 13). Habits and Home | Decluttering and Systems for ADHD Moms. https://habitsandhome.com/minimalist-tips-   clutter-free-bathroom-storage/

Amazon.com: PantryChic Smart Storage System - Starter Kit - Automatically Measures & Dispenses from Storage Containers with Digital Scale Accuracy - Kitchen & Pantry Organization & Storage: Home & Kitchen . (2024). Amazon.com. https://www.amazon.com/PantryChic-Smart- Storage-System-automatically/dp/B089P22LLX

JALG TV Stands. (n.d.). *How to design minimalist home spaces with style & comfort* . Retrieved from https://jalg.me/blogs/news/how-to-design-minimalist-home-spaces-with-style-comfort

MSN . (2024). Msn.com. https://www.msn.com/ en-us/lifestyle/cleaning-and-organizing/kitchen- organization-hacks/ar-BB1lG0gn

Maximize Vertical Space for Clutter-Free Bathrooms - SofaSpectacular . (2024, July 30). Everything Inc. https://sofaspectacular.co.uk/ maximize-vertical-space-for-clutter-free- bathrooms/

Muhammad Arsalan. (2024, October 27). *How To Create A Minimalist Living Space - Mr. Plan Publication - Medium* . Medium; Mr. Plan Publication. https://medium.com/mr-plan- publication/how-to-create-a-minimalist-living- space-995dbe8d8d68

Perman, M. (2008, November 6). *How to Get Your Email Inbox to Zero Every Day - What's Best Next.* What's Best Next. https://www.whatsbestnext.com/2008/11/how-to-get-your-email-inbox-to-zero-every-day/

Slenker-Smith, A. (2023, February 13). *How to Improve Your Sleep with a Clutter-Free Bedroom* . Simply Enough. https://www.simplyenough.net/ goodnight/

isense, my. (2024, May 6). *How to Declutter Your Bedroom for Better Sleep* Isense https://www.myisense.com/blogs/blog/how-to-declutter- your-

bedroom-for-better-sleep?srsltid=AfmBOooupc-
Eif1kVWrvd10BtRT4cDEQsOLvZXSTQpitA3i9zaCC sUch

(2022). Wayfair.com. https://www.wayfair.com/ keyword.php?
keyword=entryway+coat+and+shoe+storage

(2024). Monstersalesusa.com. https:// monstersalesusa.com/innovative-
space-solutions- exploring-the-beauty-of-hidden-storage-in-home-
design/

(2024). Thefurnestry.com. https:// thefurnestry.com/The-Rise-of-
Multifunctional- Furniture:-Transforming-Spaces-with-Versatility?
srsltid=AfmBOoqk2E5-
F_dUxNXB0nBXVa5RNOnaVUK8HwtUBABiCaw6 6fkrL6l_

*Amazon.com: Barnyatoh Shoe Storage Cabinet,Farmhouse Shoe Organizer
with 4 Flip Drawers & Barn Door Design,Freestanding Hidden Slim Narrow Shoe
Rack Cabinet for Entryway,Foyer,Hallway,Antique White : Home & Kitchen*
(2024). Amazon.com. https:// www.amazon.com/Barnyatoh-Farmhouse-
Organizer-Freestanding-Entryway/dp/ B0CTQRRX5T

*Amazon.com: Smart Design Over The Door Adjustable Pantry Organizer
Rack w/ 6 Adjustable Shelves - Steel Metal - Hanging - Wall Mount - Cans,
Spice, Storage, Closet - Kitchen [White] : Home & Kitchen* . (2024).
Amazon.com. https:// www.amazon.com/Smart-Design-Adjustable-
Organizer-Shelves/dp/B00683MM9K

Bern, L. (2020, August 30). *21 Best Hidden Storage Ideas, Stairs, Kitchens,
Bathrooms* . Laurel Home. https://laurelberninteriors.com/21-best-hidden-
storage-ideas-stairs-kitchens-bathrooms/

Door organizer Storage & Organization at Lowes.com (2024). Lowe's.
https:// www.lowes.com/pl/storage-organization/door-
organizer/4294936624-3650073036

Turn.am. (2024, May 2). *Multifunctional Furniture: Enhancing Space
Efficiency and Style* . The Best Services of Armenia in One Place; Turn.am.

https://turn.am/en/article/ multifunctional-furniture-space-saving-elegance

Antonia. (2024, August 10). *How Minimalism Can Help Messy People Find Peace* . BALANCE through SIMPLICITY. https://balancethroughsimplicity.com/minimalism-mess/

Ep 233: How to Organize Your Life When You're Not an Organized Person - Allie Casazza . (2021, September 22). Allie Casazza. https://alliecasazza.com/shownotes/233/

Legit Benefits Of Minimalism And Living With Less. (n.d.). Www.miadanielle.com. https://www.miadanielle.com/blog/benefits-of-minimalism

Organized With Kids. (2019, March 25). *How To Create a Simple Decluttering Routine - Organized With Kids.* Organized with Kids. https://organizedwithkids.com/how-to-create-a-simple- decluttering-routine/

SMART SPENDING FOR FINANCIAL WELLNESS. (2024). ResearchGate. https://doi.org/10.13140/ RG.2.2.27033.22881

Zen Decluttering Methods . (2023). Trimbox.io. https://www.trimbox.io/blog/zen-decluttering- methods

debbiecrawford. (2024, October 23). *A Minimalist's Guide to Mindful Shopping & Conscious Consumerism | Fleurish Collective* . Fleurish Collective. https://www.fleurishcollective.com/ mindful-shopping-guide/zenhabits. (2008, November 19). *Living Simply: The Ultimate Guide to Conquering Your Clutter* . Zen Habits. https://zenhabits.net/living-simply- the-ultimate-guide-to-conquering-your-clutter/

Gordon, S. (2023, April 3). *Mental Health Benefits of Cleaning and Decluttering* . Verywell Mind. https://www.verywellmind.com/how-mental- health-and-cleaning-are-connected-5097496

Minimalism in the Workplace: Streamlining Design for Enhanced Focus . (n.d.). Ocee & Four Design. https://oceefour.com/news/minimalism- in-the-workplace-streamlining-design-for- enhanced-focus/

Porter-Blake, E. (2023, July 10). *Less is More: Unlocking the Power of Minimalism in Offices* . Haiken. https://www.haiken.com/insights/ unlocking-the-power-of-minimalism

Pullein, C. (2020, March 4). *The Productivity- Boosting Benefits Of A Clean And Organised Workspace.* Medium. https://medium.com/carl- pullein/the-productivity-boosting-benefits-of-a-   clean-and-organised-workspace-cf7edaf5773

Sander, L. (2019, March 25). *The Case for Finally Cleaning Your Desk* . Harvard Business Review. https://hbr.org/2019/03/the-case-for-finally-cleaning-your-desk

The Clutter-Depression-Anxiety Cycle: How to Stop It . (2015, May 26). Nourishing Minimalism. https://nourishingminimalism.com/clutter-depression-and-anxiety-a-vicious-cycle/

(2023).   Larksuite.com. https://www.larksuite.com/en_us/topics/productivity-glossary/vision-boards

Arner Adventures. (2023, August 5). *70 Quotes About Minimalism: Embrace Simplicity and Find Meaning in Less* . Arner Adventures. https:// arneradventures.com/quotes-about-minimalism/

Journaling for Mental Health and Wellness . (2024, July 2). HelpGuide.org. https://www.helpguide.org/mental-health/wellbeing/ journaling-for-mental-health-and-wellness

Muster, V., Iran, S., & Münsch, M. (2022, August 26). *The cultural practice of decluttering as household work and its potentials for sustainable consumption* . Frontiers in Sustainability. https:// doi.org/10.3389/frsus.2022.958538

Plan to Organize. (2024, November 21). *Top 25 Inspiring Organization Quotes to Kickstart 2025.* Plan to Organize https://plantoorganize.com/ organization-quotes/

Saurabha Bhat K. (2024, January 9). *Why decluttering and organizing is important for your well-being? - Mess Minder* . Mess Minder.

https://messminder.in/why-decluttering-and-organizing- is-important-for-your-well-being/

Svitlana Popovska. (2024, November 15). *Manifest Your Goals: How Vision Board Can Help?* - XTiles. https://xtiles.app/en/blog/digital-vision- board/

Trefzger, K. (2024, April 25). *Enjoy the Rewards of a 15-Day Declutter Challenge* . Maximumgratitudeminimalstuff.com; Blogger. https://www.maximumgratitudeminimalstuff.com/ 2024/04/take-the-15-day-declutter-challenge.html

Kiernan, L. (2022, April 30). *How to Declutter Sentimental Things in a Simple and Painless Way* . The No Pressure Life | Crafts | Decor | Organization. https://www.thenopressurelife.com/ declutter-sentimental-things/

Lakes, B. (2024, October 6). *How To Develop Healthy Habits and Stick To Them This New Year* . The Lakes Treatment Center. https://www.thelakestreatmentcenter.com/blog/2024/ october/how-to-develop-healthy-habits-and-stick- to-them-/

Meyer, S., & Balasco, R. (2021, June 28). *Dealing with digital clutter: What it is and 6 places to practice digital minimalism* . Thezebra.com; The Zebra. https://www.thezebra.com/resources/ home/digital-clutter/

Waite, R. (2024, November 18). *Digital Declutter: How Minimalism Online Boosts Productivity* . Robinwaite.com; Robin Waite. https://www.robinwaite.com/blog/digital-declutter-how- minimalism-in-your-online-life-boosts- productivity-and-well-being

Coraccio, J. (2017, May 30). *Positive Mindset: Learn How to Create One & Reduce Life Clutter* . ReawakenYourBrilliance. https://reawakenyourbrilliance.com/positive-mindset- clutter-free/

Clutter-Free Mindset Training . (2023). Trimbox.io. https://www.trimbox.io/blog/clutter- free-mindset-training

English, K. (2023, December 27). *Liberating Spaces, Uplifting Souls: The Profound Emotional*

Benefits of Decluttering Your House and Life . Medium. https://kalienglish.medium.com/ liberating-spaces-uplifting-souls-the-profound- emotional-benefits-of-decluttering-your-house-

and-62a2bb133ee1

Mental health benefits of decluttering . (2021, October 25). WebMD. https://www.webmd.com/ mental-health/mental-health-benefits-of-decluttering

Schahaff, K. (2024, January 16). *"Unleash Your Radiance: The Art of Life Liberation through Decluttering."* Keisha Schahaff. https:// www.keishaschahaff.com/post/unleash-your- radiance-the-art-of-life-liberation-through- decluttering

The Many Mental Benefits of Decluttering | Psychology Today . (n.d.). Www.psychologytoday.com. https:// www.psychologytoday.com/us/blog/the-resilient- brain/202302/the-many-mental-benefits-of- decluttering

Top 10 Strategies to Stay Motivated and Achieve Goal . (2024). AFA Education Blog. https:// afaeducation.org/blog/top-10-strategies-to-stay- motivated-and-achieve-goal/

Well, D. (2023, December 6). *Understanding SMART Goals : A Guide to Crafting Achievable Objectives* . Dowellht.com; DO Well. http:// blog.dowellht.com/smart-goals

www.ingramcontent.com/pod-product-compliance
Lightning Source LLC
Chambersburg PA
CBHW070502130626
46555CB00003B/1130